MW00583381

TRANSFORMATIVE LIBRARY AND INFORMATION WORK

CHANDOS INFORMATION PROFESSIONAL SERIES

TRANSFORMATIVE LIBRARY AND INFORMATION WORK
Profiles in Social Justice

STEPHEN BALES

TINA BUDZISE-WEAVER

CP
CHANDOS
PUBLISHING
An imprint of Elsevier

ELSEVIER

Chandos Publishing is an imprint of Elsevier
50 Hampshire Street, 5th Floor, Cambridge, MA 02139, United States
The Boulevard, Langford Lane, Kidlington, OX5 1GB, United Kingdom

Copyright © 2020 Elsevier Ltd. All rights reserved.

No part of this publication may be reproduced or transmitted in any form or by any means,
electronic or mechanical, including photocopying, recording, or any information storage and
retrieval system, without permission in writing from the publisher. Details on how to seek
permission, further information about the Publisher's permissions policies and our arrangements
with organizations such as the Copyright Clearance Center and the Copyright Licensing Agency,
can be found at our website: www.elsevier.com/permissions.

This book and the individual contributions contained in it are protected under copyright by the
Publisher (other than as may be noted herein).

Notices
Knowledge and best practice in this field are constantly changing. As new research and experience
broaden our understanding, changes in research methods, professional practices, or medical
treatment may become necessary.

Practitioners and researchers must always rely on their own experience and knowledge in
evaluating and using any information, methods, compounds, or experiments described herein. In
using such information or methods they should be mindful of their own safety and the safety of
others, including parties for whom they have a professional responsibility.

To the fullest extent of the law, neither the Publisher nor the authors, contributors, or editors,
assume any liability for any injury and/or damage to persons or property as a matter of products
liability, negligence or otherwise, or from any use or operation of any methods, products,
instructions, or ideas contained in the material herein.

British Library Cataloguing-in-Publication Data
A catalogue record for this book is available from the British Library

Library of Congress Cataloging-in-Publication Data
A catalog record for this book is available from the Library of Congress

ISBN: 978-0-08-103011-0

For information on all Chandos Publishing publications
visit our website at https://www.elsevier.com/books-and-journals

Publisher: Glyn Jones
Editorial Project Manager: Joanna Collett
Production Project Manager: Debasish Ghosh
Cover Designer: Greg Harris

Typeset by MPS Limited, Chennai, India

Working together
to grow libraries in
developing countries

www.elsevier.com • www.bookaid.org

Contents

Acknowledgments

The authors thank the following people for graciously agreeing to take part in this project:

Shanel Adams, Cullen Beckhorn, Scott Bonner, Deborah Caldwell-Stone, Kevin Caplicki, Robin Champieux, Allister Chang, Ryan Clover-Owens, Lauren Comito, Ana Elisa De Campos Salles, Katie Dover-Taylor, Adam Echelman, Joshua Finnell, Jenna Freedman, Bonnie Gordon, Kelly Grogg, Sherre Harrington, Stavroula Harrissis, Katie Ishizuka, Abena Hutchful, James Larue, Edwin Lindo, Julia Lipscomb, Allison Macrina, Laura Moulton, Yusef Omowale, Andrea Perez, Peter Rachleff, Arlene Rengert, Donald Russell, Ramon Stephens, Karen Stornelli, Bonnie Tijerina, Cornelius Vango, Rebekah Walker, Dana Ward, Kenneth A. Yamashita, and Sarah Zettervall.

The authors thank Mitzi Bales for the front cover design.

Stephen Bales thanks

I would like to thank my beautiful wife Mitzi and my two reds Stella and Irene. I would like to thank Cheryl Bales and Karen Henry. Immense thanks to my co-author Tina Budzise-Weaver. I would also like to thank my colleagues at Texas A&M University Libraries Laura Sare, Associate Professor and Government Information Librarian, Derek Halling, Associate Professor and Director of Evans Subject Specialists, and Rebecca Hankins, Professor, Archivist/Librarian of Africana and Women's & Gender Studies.

Tina Budzise-Weaver thanks

I would like to thank my partner in life, Tim, and son Ethan for ignoring me on Sundays when I took time to write my chapters. I would like to thank my extended family for their love and encouragement. It was a joy to co-author with my colleague Stephen Bales on this book. I was inspired by the positive impact these organizations are making in their communities. I would also like to thank the following colleagues for their support, Laura Sare, Government Information Librarian, Texas A&M University Libraries, Pauline Melgoza, Science and Engineering Librarian, Texas A&M University Libraries, and Bruce Neville, Science and Engineering Librarian, Texas A&M University Libraries.

CHAPTER ONE

Introduction

1.1 Transformative library and information work and social justice

Modern libraries are routinely associated with social justice as well as adjunct ideas like economic justice, human rights, free access to education, and democracy. Furthermore, one often sees library and information professions as tasked with furthering such ideas, associating library workers with the role of supporting the development of patron autonomy and agency through the professional and responsible custodianship and provision of information. An increasing number of library and information science practitioners, both professional and paraprofessional (including alternatively or non-credentialed workers), as well as volunteers, are making explicit links between their own library and information work and desired social justice outcomes, questioning long held beliefs like library neutrality and professional status, as well as recognizing library work as an essentially political project. Indeed, for many library and information workers, *library practice* is becoming synonymous with *the social justice project*; i.e., it is developing into a praxis aimed squarely at positive societal transformation that works towards normative outcomes. Such outcomes frequently hinge on the goal of increasing social equity by means of focusing on the sociocultural welfare of the individual, the transformation of the larger society and its institutions, or, in many cases, both.

Many library and information workers—one might argue most all of them—work towards justice within organizations hamstrung by traditional bureaucratic and hierarchical administrative milieus that mystify, but still reflect, the biases and prejudices inherent in modern neoliberal society. Other library and information workers have, in some measure, avoided or escaped the clutches of modern institutions, working for organizations largely outside of the hegemonic malaise bolstered by dominant institutions like most public and academic libraries. Both of these types of library and information worker are important to the furtherance of social justice

Transformative Library and Information Work.
DOI: https://doi.org/10.1016/B978-0-08-103011-0.00001-0
© 2020 Elsevier Ltd.
All rights reserved.
1

related projects. Indeed, some workers successfully divide their time between both types of organizations, traditional and alternative. Those people working in the traditional institutions offer up a valuable internal critique at the same time that they serve as a valuable reformative influence. The workers at alternative or non-traditional organizations, even if they may not—at least for the present—be wholly divorced from the traditional institutions, have an excellent opportunity to experiment with emergent counter-hegemonic paradigms. Furthermore, these two spheres of information work, the orthodox and the heterodox, may look towards each other to engage in a fruitful dialogue concerning what does and does not work in the pursuit of justice. The organizations, programs, and initiatives highlighted in this book look to both of these spheres with the hope of furthering such a discourse.

1.2 Our project

This volume gathers 30 profiles of alternative, progressive, and radical library and information organizations, programs, and initiatives (hereafter referred to as transformative library and information "projects") that work towards achieving social justice—as well as related concepts such as human rights—in and for the communities they serve. *Transformative library and information work: Profiles in social justice* is a continuation of a project initiated with the book *Social justice and library work: A guide to theory and practice* (Bales, 2018). Chapter 4 of the earlier book presented seven project profiles: ARL Diversity and Leadership Programs, the 2016 Los Angeles Anarchist Book Fair, Free Government Information, Lesbian Herstory Archives, Librarians and Archivists With Palestine, Seattle Public Library Books on Bikes Program, and Occupy Wall Street Library. These vignettes provided real-world examples of social justice praxis, i.e., theory put into action, or what famed philosopher of education Freire (1970) described as "the action and reflection of men and women upon the world in order to transform it" (p. 79). The intent of relating these stories was to provide examples, inspiration, and guidance to library and information workers that might be contemplating, or may have even started, transformative library and information projects of their own. People directly involved with the seven projects, such as founders, directors, and volunteers, gave interviews providing insight into particular motivations and challenges.

Transformative library and information work continues with this model. For this book, we identified 30 projects and conducted interviews with at least one person, and sometimes groups of two or three people, intimately involved in some way with each effort. The long form interviews were open-ended and many times freewheeling, but all centered on the history, scope, and goals of the transformative projects, as well as the material realities and challenges that they faced. Participants were excited to take part, showing us the passion that had certainly gotten them involved in social justice/information related work in the first place. The process of researching, interviewing for, and writing this book was revelatory. It brought to light the impressive number of library and information work related projects happening today as well as the great range of change-making activities taking place through them.

1.3 The rest of the book

The profiles herein range in length from approximately 1300 to 2500 words. We contacted a person, usually a project's founder or coordinator, for interviews. In many instances, other people also gave interviews. This turned out to be a welcomed occurrence when it happened, as the additional voices added depth to our understanding of the projects. Following each profile are three to five bulleted "Takeaways" that summarize the major points or ideas covered in the body of the narrative. Although several of the projects discussed in this book are international in scope, we chose to focus only on those projects with offices or representatives in the United States. We did this largely for logistical reasons, finding it prohibitively difficult to obtain institutional review board authorization for a representative sample of worldwide projects. Future book projects, however, may expand upon what we have started here to include coverage of other countries and geographical areas.

In addition to this introduction, the book consists of three chapters containing project profiles: (2) Organize: Transformative Libraries and Archives; (3) Advocate: Transformative Library and Information Projects Reaching Out; and (4) Connect and Transmit: Organizations for Professional Support and Outlets for Professional Communication. The use of transitive verbs for each of the chapter headings is intentional. We approached this volume applying a basic philosophy of action. That is, we viewed reality as material in motion as opposed to an outlook that relies on empty abstractions. The yappy generation of ideas for their sake only, and without material application, is a masturbatory act. We are, therefore, not idealists in the philosophical sense, but in the sense that we see efforts in pursuit of normative goals as necessary and transformational. A dialectical, progressive view of existence holds *doing* and *becoming* as axial; i.e., change is reality and vice versa. The transformative information projects covered exemplify this notion. Every one of them focuses on *doing* things, on implementing positive societal changes through activities underpinned by ideas, through praxis. The subjects of this book are all transformative in the positive sense. Not only are they always *becoming* something new, they are all dedicated to *remaking* a society into one that is more fair and equitable.

That said, the division of the profiles into Chapters Two, Three, and Four is somewhat arbitrary. One might justify including many of the profiles in one or both of the other two chapters. For example, Slab City Library (see page 49), an anarchist community library serving a squatter/snowbird community in the Sonoran desert of Southern California is included in Chapter Two, "Organize: Transformative Collections" when it might have just as easily been placed in Chapter Three, "Advocate: Transformative Library and Information Projects Reaching Out" instead. We have chosen to place cases such as Slab City Library in the chapter that we feel best reflects the focus of the individual profile. For Slab City Library, we chose to focus primarily on the library itself, i.e., how it is run, what it contains, etc. That is not to say that we ignore issues surrounding its community of patrons. Following is a brief outline for the rest of the book.

1.4 Chapter 2: Organize: transformative libraries and archives

This chapter collects 12 profiles of projects based on collections of information. They are, again, much more than just these collections. They transcend the material and electronic collections, becoming community centers, change agents, and prefigurative information projects that challenge and resist dominant ideologies and structures. None would claim neutrality. Some even serve alcohol.

1.5 Chapter 3: Advocate: transformative library and information projects reaching out

This chapter collects 13 profiles covering transformative endeavors that serve the needs (informational and otherwise) of a variety of different populations, many of them being at-risk groups. The projects range from the relatively large (e.g., Libraries without Borders, National Coalition against Censorship) to the quite modest (e.g., Laundromat Library League, Whole Person Librarianship). Regardless of size, they all use innovative methods and strategies to serve the interests of their constituencies.

1.6 Chapter 4: Connect and transmit: organizations for professional support and outlets for professional communication

The final chapter collects five profiles of organizations and outlets for communication that seek to connect information workers. Three profiles, Allied Media Conference: Radical Libraries, Archives, and Museums Track; Urban Librarians Conference; and Joint Conference of Librarians of Color, put on innovative conference programs for transformative library and information workers. The remaining two projects, Feminist Task Force of the American Library Association's Social Responsibilities Round Table and Rainbow Round Table, connect and advocate for information workers who are members of these marginalized groups (women and LGBTQIA +) (lesbian, gay, bisexual, transgender, pansexual, genderqueer, queer, intersex, agender, asexual, and ally) as well as coordinate efforts for at-risk user populations.

1.7 A note concerning terminology

The previous book, *Social justice and library work* uses the term "library work" as an inclusive way to "encompass all tasks, both physical and mental, that propel the library as a sociocultural institution, as well as to realize the library's humanistic potential in modern society" (Bales,

2018, p. 1). Correspondingly, "library worker" was substituted for "'librarian' (unless the distinction is necessary) to identify all of those people that labor to realize the above tasks: professional librarians and related information professionals like archivists and museum curators, paraprofessional staff members, technical support staff, and volunteers" (p. 1). The impetus for these choices in terminology sprang largely from a spirit of post-professionalism that seeks to bridge the gap between people who, besides structurally imposed and arguably elitist professional divisions, all work towards common goals. While many of the organizations profiled in the present volume may self-identify as libraries, others do not. As a result we have decided to be, when possible, even more liberal in the terminology that we adopt, using "library and information work" and "library and information worker" unless a more specific term like "librarian" or "library worker" is needed for clarity.

References

Bales, S. (2018). *Social justice and library work: A guide to theory and practice*. Cambridge, MA: Chandos Publishing.

Freire, P. (1970). *Pedagogy of the oppressed* (M. B. Ramos, Trans.). New York: Continuum.

CHAPTER TWO

Organize: transformative libraries and archives

2.1 Introduction

This chapter profiles 11 transformative library and information work related projects that maintain collections with strong focuses on social justice and/or related issues like feminism or radical politics, make available tools for social transformation to their patrons, or do both:

1. ABC NO Rio Zine Library
2. Anarchy Archives
3. Barnard Zine Library
4. Bellingham Alternative Library
5. Conscious Kid
6. Durland Alternatives Library
7. East Side Freedom Library
8. Estelita's Library
9. Interference Archive
10. Provisions Library
11. Slab City Library
12. Southern California Library for Social Studies and Research

The ways in which these organizations make their collections available to their patrons is wonderfully diverse. For instance, Estelita's Library, Seattle's "Justice Focused Community Library," is an intimate neighborhood library/bookstore with a small collection of about 2000 print books focusing on radical political theory, liberation struggles, race, gender, and sexual identity, as well as other social justice related topics (it also has a wine and beer bar!). Proprietor Edwin Lindo said that he wanted to make Estelita's cozy, tight, and small, realizing that doing so helped his mission to make the place a welcoming community gathering point and catalyst for change. That is not to say that Estelita's neighborhood vibe has hurt its reach; twenty percent of its subscribing members are people living outside of Seattle and Lindo said, "There is a critical mass over every economic and

Transformative Library and Information Work.
DOI: https://doi.org/10.1016/B978-0-08-103011-0.00002-2
© 2020 Elsevier Ltd.
All rights reserved.

racial makeup." At the other end of the format spectrum, Anarchy Archives was born digital as a tool to supplement founder Dana Ward's popular Pitzer College course "Anarchy and the Internet," and remains one of the oldest continuously operating full-text archives of anarchist related materials on the World Wide Web. And Slab City Library, which serves a Southern California squatter community in the Sonoran Desert, is many different things: a library, a community center, a movie theater, a music venue, an art installation, a bar (again demonstrating an apparent connection between transformative collections and alcoholic beverages), and more.

The organizations in this chapter also represent different levels of time commitment on the part of people we interviewed. For many participants, their transformative library and information work was also their full time job. For Slab City Libraries' Cornelius Vango, the work is more than a full time job; the library is the realization of ongoing art project and is Vango's home. Other people we interviewed, like Julia Lipscomb, ABC No Rio's zine librarian, work on a volunteer basis in addition to full-time employment elsewhere. What came across in everyone interviewed, however, was the great amount of dedication shared for social justice work and a deep recognition of *the power of the collection* for both organizing and supplementing positive change.

Before continuing, it is important to remember that this book's organization of transformative information organizations is ultimately a conceit. When we approached Peter Rachleff, co-founder and co-executive director of St. Paul, Minnesota's East Side Freedom Library (ESFL) for an interview, he was leery of the book relegating ESFL to the status of "just a collection." ESFL is, Rachleff told us, so much more than a collection. The same may be said for the other projects profiled here, many of which may have easily been fit into Chapter 3. Therefore, even though every project here is notable for its collection, we use that collection as a touchpoint to give context for the great variety of people, and projects that these projects encompass.

2.2 ABC No Rio Zine Library: with Julia Lipscomb, Zine Librarian (Sept. 13, 2018)

http://www.abcnorio.org/facilities/zine_library.html; zine@abcnorio.org

Zines—the term is a shortened form of "fanzines"—are limited-circulation, small press (indeed, many zines are handmade), non-commercial print magazines, booklets, or pamphlets that may concentrate on a potentially limitless variety of topics including music, art, poetry, literature, politics, and personal life and opinion ("perzines"). They tend to focus on specialized and niche topics, many of which have no equivalent resources coming out of commercial presses. There are, for example, zines dedicated to computer hacking, knitting, anarcho-syndicalism, addiction, and sobriety. A recurring denominator among zines is these publications' intensely personal nature; not only do their creators usually control "all aspects of the production process: from the content, to the design and layout, to production (usually by photocopier), to distribution" (Groeneveld, 2016, p. 1), they many times offer intimate windows into the minds and lives of their authors. This is, unsurprisingly, not a medium of expression where financial gain is a primary object, or even an object at all. Rather, the zines' creators are driven by motivations like artistic passion, intellectual curiosity, activism, or simply a deep-seated interest in their particular subject. Some examples of zines include the iconic punk rock forum *Maximum RocknRoll, Filmme Fatales,* which looks at cinema using feminism as a prism, *Slug and Lettuce*, a resource guide for the punk and Do-it-yourself (DIY) communities, *Bitch,* an outlet for third-wave feminist thought, and *The Tenth*, which focuses on the queer Black community in New York City. There are thousands of these publications dating back to the 1930s, many of which are hard to find because of their ephemeral nature, small print runs, and sometimes-capricious distribution. They are unique, however, in the way that they speak to their readers, making connections and community in ways that commercial publications rarely do. Nevertheless, because of their ephemeral nature and amateur production and distribution, zines are regularly overlooked by traditional libraries. Thankfully, this inattention appears to be on the wane with the emergence of a new wave of zine conscious information workers in traditional library environments as well as the success of curated collections such as the ABC No Rio Zine Library (hereafter referred to as the "Zine Library").

ABC No Rio is a non-profit, collectively run center for art and activism located in New York City. Founded in 1980 at 156 Rivington Street, a tenement building on the Lower East Side that formerly housed artists, the organization derived its name from what was left of the dilapidated sign out front, which had originally read "Abogado Con Notario." ABC No Rio has persevered nearly 30 years in the face of both government pressure against squatters and East Village gentrification efforts that have resulted in the displacement of local residents. During this time, it has become a central node for the NYC art, punk rock, and DIY scenes: communities that may run counter to, and oftentimes come into conflict with, the dominant cultural and political paradigms. The place is legendary for its weekly "HardCore/Punk Matinee" shows and its art exhibitions. In addition to these hallmark activities, it provides a number of free or low cost services for members of the community that support creative expression and social and political activism. These initiatives, all of which are run by volunteers, include a computer center, a photography darkroom, a print shop, and a zine library. Together they support a commitment to "social justice, equality, anti-authoritarianism, autonomous action, collective processes, and to nurturing alternative structures and institutions operating on such principles" (ABC No Rio, n.d.). By offering such opportunities, ABC No Rio has become a communication touchpoint for its many-times underserved and misunderstood constituencies. The Zine Library does much to help realize this function through its archive, becoming a nexus for the spread of ideas and a tool for the crystallization of community.

Embracing the potential of the zine format as a catalytic medium for positive social change, community building, and the representation and dissemination of unconventional, emerging, and underrepresented viewpoints, the Zine Library began its work in 1998 with ABC No Rio's acquisition of the Blackout Zine Library, a small collection of approximately 2000 items. The Blackout Books (a former infoshop on the Lower East Side) collection had been donated to ABC No Rio by a squat in the South Bronx then undergoing eviction by the city. Since its start, ABC No Rio's collection has grown rapidly and currently contains over 13,000 items. Julia Lipscomb, one of the Zine Library's two volunteer open-hours librarians, explained that the collection reflects the nature of ABC No Rio as an organization: "We are a very political, left-leaning organization, and a lot of the zines have to do with politics and punk. They really run the gamut of just about everything, but we are most known for anti-authoritarianism and punk." Underneath and in addition to this broad topical umbrella, the Zine Library's collection covers a range of subjects, with major collecting areas including international politics, anti-authoritarianism, anti-fascism, anti-racism, housing rights, feminism, New York history, music, and DIY. It is also one of few such collections to collect zines printed on newsprint.

Although the zine collection is non-circulating—loaning out the items would be ill-advised because of their often delicate nature and rarity—it is by no means an airless museum or archive. The collection is meant to be used by community members and anyone else with an interest or need in the collection. Lipscomb commented on the broad range of people that the Zine Library serves, noting that:

> [The community is comprised of] people from grassroots, DIY networks, and those adults that have had a history in these scenes and people from New York, Lower Manhattan, and people from different zine communities as well. These are very New York based communities, but then there are international tourists too. [...] Researchers and undergraduate students [also] come and visit us, and people from colleges both in New York and traveling from Europe and other different parts of the country. We get librarians that are interested in zines, and some visitors who are thinking of making a zine and want to get some inspiration.

This is a disparate group of people. Bartel (2004) echoed this description of "zinester" community in her book *From A to zine: Building a winning zine collection in your library*, writing that zinesters are not a monolithic group and, although many adopt punk or alternative lifestyles, many do not. The zine community thrives on this diversity; it is, and it should remain, an essential element of its character. Dedicated zinesters as well as interested casual readers are drawn to a form of media that validates individuality and, as a result, helps to validate them.

Herein lies the power of the medium, zines are powerful tools that can help to create and bind communities, bringing together many different types of people from marginalized backgrounds and fringe communities. Although the process of reading and writing are intensely personal experiences, zines are special in that they foster relationships, creating "intimate, affectionate connections between their creators and readers, not just communities but embodied communities that are made possible by the materiality of the zine medium" (Freedman, 2006, p. 214). Their intimate nature is, as Wertham (1973) wrote, perfect for connecting small groups in ways that mass communication cannot through mass media's "fetishism of large numbers [that] has left communication gaps and empty spaces" (p. 129). Writing on the connection between zines and riot grrrl feminist punk culture, Buchanan (2018) also noted this community building power, arguing that zines' production and distribution helps to shape communities that actively resist dominant power structures and narratives (p. 44).

By virtue of its inherent diversity, zine communities, as well as the communities that they support, tend towards egalitarianism. Such egalitarianism is reflected in the composition of the Zine Library itself, which consists totally of volunteers and operates on a consensus model.

The operating committee is a small group, but one that is agile and responsive. It is composed of a fluid but ardent group of volunteers that, while loosely organized, understands the power of the zine for knitting together community because they are in that community.

> The most active members now are about five to six right now. There are a few others that are on the email list, and they can respond to different outreach efforts and events if they choose too. We have a group email. It is not super active. We probably communicate, send out messages about events and things maybe about once a month, once every other month—you will hear from somebody on the Zine Library list. This is a way to communicate if we have an opening and we are looking for somebody who might be interested in filling in for a shift. So if a zine librarian cannot make it that night or if we have different outreach events planned [. . .] we will use the groups to communicate [. . .].

When queried about the major obstacles faced by the Zine Library, Lipscomb was upbeat. While the majority of obstacles have been faced by the ABC No Rio organization in toto and concern its battle for existence in the face of outside pressure, the Zine Library, she said, had encountered surprisingly few obstacles besides, as described below, its temporary relocation due to the construction of a new building. It is with great relief, however, that for the time being, the organization, including the Zine Library and ABC No Rio's other initiatives, is able to operate "in exile," remaining open but working out of nearby rental space. Lipscomb suggested that it is good for zine collections to develop a focus, to apply a measured subjectivity when building a collection towards a community, and to aim at being inclusive yet unique. The Zine Library, for instance, is geared towards the DIY community, and carefully considers glossy art or poetry zines before adding them to the collection. Lipscomb said that looking at the bigger picture, and looking at other zine libraries, is a good tool for developing a unique identity.

As of this writing, the Zine Library is going through major changes. Lipscomb said that the original building at 156 Rivington is currently "a hole in the ground," having been torn down to make room for a new building funded completely by donation. As part of a deal struck with the city government, and representing a major win for ABC No Rio, the organization was able to purchase the property at 156 Rivington for one dollar by agreeing to bring it up to code. Although many community members are deeply saddened by the loss of the old building, a 17th century era building that had become iconic in the NYC art and punk scenes, ABC No Rio's success and stability demonstrate both its steadfastness and the ability of such organizations, i.e., those transformative collectives working outside of the mainstream, to beat the odds and operate effectively in modern capitalist societies.

Traditional libraries, be they public, academic or school libraries, would do well to look to the Zine Library as a guide. Bartel (2004) acknowledged the power of zines to serve alienated cultures, as well as the duty of libraries and library workers of all types to do this:

> Zines add depth and scope to library collections, offering patrons a diversity of style, content, and subject matter unparalleled elsewhere. Strong collections are built through diversity, and zines offer information and viewpoints which no other form can duplicate. Moreover, zines are personal—without the filters of publisher, editors, and critics—and many patrons crave the unprocessed experience they offer (pp. 28–33).

While the radical politics, horizontal organization, and egalitarianism of ABC No Rio is a hard sell to most traditional libraries, places where patriarchal organizational structures and a current fascination with capitalist business models has rendered things like these to be mostly aspirational, the Zine Library demonstrates the importance of publicly accessible collections of touchable, relatable materials celebrating diversity and individuality.

Julia Lipscomb is an artist and zine librarian currently living in Queens, NY. She volunteers weekly at ABC No Rio Zine Library. Previously she was involved in grassroots arts and zine communities in Seattle and Spokane, WA before moving to New York to gain a Master in Arts & Culture Management at Pratt Institute. Outside of the Zine Library, Julia works in customer service and strives to bring that same hospitality to Zine Library open hours.

2.2.1 Takeaways

- Think of sources outside of the traditional press when building collections. For every commercial magazine there may be multiple zines that will attract readers as well as inspire them to create their own publications.
- The writing and reading of alternative press materials both builds community and cements it. A zine collection provides a focal point for community building.
- Many people reading zines may be members of marginalized groups. Information workers have a duty to provide information to such groups that they both desire and need.

2.3 Anarchy Archives: with Dana Ward, Founder (Sept. 21, 2018)

http://dwardmac.pitzer.edu/anarchist_archives/; dward@pitzer.edu

Anarchists have long understood the power of written language to support and transmit their ideas (see Bales, 2018, pp. 147–151 for a profile of the Los Angeles Book Fair). Anarchist bibliophilia is demonstrated by the large number of small press anarchist publishers (e.g., AK Press), bookstores, and info-shops presently in operation, and these organizations have only been increasing over the past several decades. Anarchists also have a rich history of publishing in small press and, more recently, through Do-it-yourself publications like zines. There are libraries and archives dedicated to collecting anarchist literature, most notably London's Kate Sharpley Library (there is now also a physical location in California) as well as the emergence of smaller libraries and archives such as Saint Paul, Minnesota's Eastside Freedom Library (see p. 33) and Southern California's Slab City Library (see p. 49). In general, however, the "troubled history of many activists (subjected to searches, repeatedly imprisoned, exiled, etc.) has certainly not lent itself to the easy growth of archives and personal collections" (Balsamini, 2012, pp. 1–2). Many of the existing anarchist collections are part of larger libraries and archives such as the Labadie Collection at the University of Michigan, the University of Victoria's Anarchist Archive, the Hoover Institute, and New York University's Tamiment Library and Robert F. Washer Labor Archives. The limitations on accessibility that housing the primarily physical collections at such institutions inevitably privileges their academic use over their ready availability to many activists, as well as restricts the collection's usage to what is effectively an academic elite with access to the library or archive's materials through their institutional memberships. Library and information workers at such places, furthermore, may have an inaccurate understanding of political anarchism, seeing it as a doctrine of chaos that idealizes a complete lack of organization, when this could not be further from the truth. This ignorance is remarkable, considering that anarchism has a long modern history. Smaller, independent anarchist libraries and archives often also suffer a similar problem in terms of the lack of ease of access for, as Moran (2016) noted, they are many times located offline in private residences or anarchist meeting spaces. The Internet and World Wide Web, however, have not only given activists and researchers—and with anarchism the lines between these two categories are often blurred—outlets for publishing and disseminating anarchist and related radical information, but provided them with new ways to both archive the materials and make them more easily accessible to larger, as well as more geographically dispersed, audiences. One such successful online archive is the Anarchy Archives housed at Pitzer College, a member of the Claremont Colleges Consortium, started by Pitzer Political Studies Professor Dana Ward in 1995.

Anarchy Archives' approach to providing the public with anarchist information is simple and effective. The bulk of the material consists of a free digital collection of anarchist writings in a section titled "The Cynosure." This section includes digital versions of nearly all of the complete works published by the major anarchist figures of the nineteenth and twentieth centuries such as Mikhail Bakunin, Emma Goldman, Enrico Malatesta, Noam Chomsky, and Peter Kropotkin. Along with the collected work of each author, there are related biographies, bibliographies, commentaries, and images. Materials from minor anarchists—"Bright but Lesser Lights"—are also included but many are not as complete as the collections of the major anarchists. The works are provided in the original English or are given in English translation, with many of the collection's translations done by Anarchy Archives itself. There are also large numbers of works in foreign languages that have not yet been translated, including many in French and Spanish. Another section, "Cold Off the Presses" is a trove of digitized anarchist pamphlets and periodicals such as the *Social Revolutionary Anarchist Federation Bulletin, Regeneración,* and *Zero: Anarcha-Feminist Monthly.* The third major section of the archives, "Anarchist History," includes historical summaries on events such as the Paris Commune, the Haymarket Massacre, and the Spanish Civil War, as well as other valuable tools for researchers like images, a bibliography, and a timeline.

Anarchy Archives started out as part of a course taught by Ward, "Anarchy and the Internet." The online project, he said, began as a pedagogical tool for his students by which they would mark up and make available radical writings: "The students had to turn in something they did every week, and a lot of students did translations. So we translated [nineteenth century French anarchist] Pierre-Joseph Proudhon's letters that have never been translated from French to English." Some semesters Ward had over 60 students each producing weekly contributions. At the same time that it engaged with anarchist material, the project recalled an anarchist history that connects publishing to education while making its participants a part of that history:

> Many anarchists were printers and typesetters, and that is how they got their education. Proudhon was a typesetter and educated himself as a byproduct of setting type. I got the idea that students could learn about anarchism by marking up text of the anarchists and making them available to the public so that other people could have access to material that was inaccessible in any other way.

Another nineteenth century anarchist that Ward looked to for inspiration in developing Anarchy Archives is Élisée Reclus, who was also probably the foremost European geographer of the second half of the nineteenth century. For Ward, Reclus

> [. . .] represented to me kind of an academic and an activist alike... You know, he combined his activism with his academic work. He was part of the Paris Commune and was arrested and so forth. Darwin actually came to his defense. His philosophy was that geography shapes social relations, and in a way the geography of the Internet shapes social relations. So, his is an inspiring model.

In addition to its obvious connection with the course content, using the Internet as a platform for providing access to anarchist thought seemed to be a natural outlet for the project. The Internet, Ward said, "is in many ways an anarchist organization." There is no overarching authority, people enter and exit at will, and they are free to post pretty much what they want. The Internet, he continued,

> had a tremendous impact [on anarchism]. It has made many more people aware of anarchism than otherwise would have been [. . .] I think there is a pretty clear line between exposure to anarchist ideas and the emergence of a much stronger anarchist movement after the WTO [World Trade Organization] demonstrations of the late 1990s.

Besides the huge volume of information on Anarchy Archives, the site is notable for its remarkable longevity. The site is the oldest continuously run and freely available collection of its type on the Web, having been online for almost 25 years. Although the online environment is conducive to the spread of information, the medium is not particularly known for the longevity of any of the resources available, anarchist or not. Add to the tenuousness of existence on the Web the fact that many online anarchist projects are collectives, which may be short-lived, and many online collections often fail to be updated or simply disappear. For instance, the SPUNK Library, which was well known among online anarchists, was last updated in 2002 (Spunk Collective, 2002). Anarchy Archives, however, has had the benefit of firm institutional support (a remarkable feat for a free collection of anarchist materials). Ward cited this support as one reason for its impressive longevity: "Pitzer is a very progressive institution. The faculty run the place. We do not have administrators that block things like this. They gave me research money. They paid to provide for unlimited server capacity and so forth." The site's popularity among activists and scholars is also noteworthy. Although it is difficult to say exactly who is using Anarchy Archives (the site counter went down years ago), Pitzer College has informed Ward that the archives gets more traffic than any other page on the institution's Web presence. Ward said that people are using the page to locate materials that they cannot find easily any place else, and that anarchist literature from the site has made its way across the Web: "if you find a classic anarchist work on the Internet, even if it is on another site, it probably came from [the Archives]. People are copying it, spreading it out, and that is another way that the material circulates."

Even though Ward retired from Pitzer College in 2012, he continues to teach the course that got Anarchy Archives going, and which has been renamed "Anarchist History and Thought." He also continues to do maintenance on the site and add new material. The Anarchy Archives' contents continue to grow even though finding additional material to put online is becoming increasingly more difficult: "We have got all the low lying fruit, but there is still much more work to be done." When asked for possible tips to give those individuals or organizations that might be thinking about the creation of a similar online collection of radical materials, Ward said that one should be prepared for incredibly time-consuming and tedious work. Machines, Ward said, are "good but they are not perfect."

Dana Ward is Professor Emeritus of Political Studies at Pitzer College, part of the Claremont Colleges consortium. Anarchy Archives is the product of a dozen years teaching "Anarchist History and Thought," in which students turned anarchist material into digitized formats to be made available for free on the World Wide Web. Ward spent over three decades at Pitzer, during which time he also taught for the Johns Hopkins-Nanjing University Center for Chinese and American Studies, Ankara University, and Miyazaki International College. In retirement he spends half the year in Claremont and the other on his homestead in Unity, Maine.

2.3.1 Takeaways

- Take advantage of the power of the Internet to free radical information that might otherwise remain siloed by geographical limitations.
- Even though financial support is never easy to find, even traditional institutions like colleges and universities may be convinced of the value of maintaining radical collections. Identify such progressive institutions for possible funding opportunities.
- The work may be time-consuming and tedious, but you might be able to incorporate it into other projects to help accomplish the task and fill two needs at once.

2.4 Barnard Zine Library: with Jenna Freedman, Zine Librarian (Sept. 1, 2018)

3009 Broadway, New York, NY 10027, (212)-854-3953
https://zines.barnard.edu/; zines@barnard.edu

Established in 1889, Barnard College is one of the oldest colleges in New York City to first admit women. The selective academic institution educates more than 2500 undergraduates, empowering them to become leaders in "the arts, business, government, science, and as activists for various causes" (Barnard College, 2018). To further this goal, Zine Librarian Jenna Freedman has amassed over 11,000 zines in the college's Zine Library, a collection focusing on feminism and femme identity.

Even though her father is a librarian, Freedman took her own path to library work. She obtained a theater degree but decided to pursue her love of books, bookstores, and libraries after enduring a "particularly harrowing season of Shakespeare in the Park." Freedman found that, in contrast to a busy production schedule as a theatrical technician, "where everything was urgent but nothing was important," libraries took the opposite approach, i.e., they were places where "everything was important but nothing was urgent." Soon after Freedman started her job as Coordinator of Reference Services at Barnard Library, she presented the idea of a zine collection to her library dean. She had first encountered zines in the 1990s through immersion in spoken word performances, poetry, and fiction. However, after meeting zine author Celia C. Perez in library school, Freedman became captivated with the political and personal writings that construct the journeys of many zine authors. She pitched the idea of a zine library centered on women's studies, emphasizing the value of developing a niche collection of zines written by women (cis- and transgender) with an emphasis on zines by Women of Color (WOC) (Barnard Zines Library, 2018).

Zines are independently produced publications that are often self-printed and handmade taking the form of pamphlets, stapled booklets, and distributed indifferent to profit. Hays (2017) wrote that zines generally have a readership or community in mind and tend to "address a known or assumed community of readers, allow the writer to consciously construct her self-identity on the page, and allow for a visual representation of (un)certainty through an intentionally unfinished published text" (p. 92). She noted that women-authored zines seek to create a space where their voices on political and personal self-expression can be heard, and that the rise of underground punk rock culture contributed the core anticapitalistic and Do-It-Yourself (DIY) ethics that have become an attribute of feminist zine creation (Hays, 2017). These DIY personal texts are born out of the "third wave feminist rebellion against male domination of punk" (Freedman, 2009, p. 53), and "riot grrl" zines blossomed in the nineties with publications like *Action Girl Newsletter, Jigsaw,* and *Bikini Kill,* enabling women to voice their personal perceptions of society, politics, and music. They are an expression of confidence, anger, intelligence, and, above all, self-identified emotion that does not permeate the monolithic mass media landscape.

Barnard Zine Library describes the zines in their collection as "personal and political publications on activism, anarchism, body image, third wave feminism, gender, parenting, queer community, riot grrrl, sexual assault, trans experience, and other topics" (Barnard Zines Library, 2018). As the collection has grown, Freedman said that the project's mission has evolved to "explicitly recognize people of all genders who are writing about feminism or femme identity." Inspired by her close friend Celia C. Perez, Freedman said that Perez's work greatly informed her decision to tailor the Barnard Zine Collection to WOC:

> Her zines are just wonderful and I think [they] inspired me. One thing that is kind-of nice from the very beginning is the Barnard Zine Library's emphasis on zines by women of color. That might have been partially because I got into zines through a WOC, so I hope that my relationship and knowledge about race, ethnicity, bigotry in general, and oppression have grown and deepened since I first founded the collection.

After getting permission to proceed in 2003, Freedman carefully considered how to build the collection, asking advice from legendary Wisconsin Historical Society librarian and then Barnard archivist James Danky, as well as others. Based on Danky's advice, she created a system where one copy of each zine goes into a climate controlled archives, while the library makes a second copy available for circulation and interlibrary loan. Columbia University Libraries hosts the zine records in their online public access catalog, but they are also in WorldCat, making them discoverable to the world. Two student workers assist with writing abstracts for the zines in preparation for cataloging. Making the items more widely accessible has not only opened the collection to the campus community but also local and international researchers, Girl Scout troops, and junior high school students.

The campus has developed a vibrant zine culture. In 2010, Freedman and a student worker, Jennie Rose Halperin (now also a professional library worker) launched the Barnard Zine Club to encourage campus level buy-in and invite students to take ownership of the zine collection. Club members construct a zine each semester and add their own work to the growing collection. Therefore, not only do members use the existing collection, they take part in its creation. In addition to Freedman's efforts to encourage zine culture at Barnard, the campus has also seen the success of the New York City Feminist Zinefest, held annually at the college since its second iteration in 2014 and giving attendees the opportunity to be part of a safe and welcoming space to share their common interests. As the interest in zines grows, she cautions students to ask zine creators' permission to utilize their work and be respectful of their personal writings. Freedman said that respecting zinesters

> ...is really just good manners and a lot of the stuff that I do as a special collections librarian are common sense things that are motivated out of "a do unto others" kind-of rule or just my own internal code of ethics. But it turns out treating people well is good for your collection. They are more likely to trust you, and doing the outreach introduces you to people. I may have asked someone what pronouns they use, and two years later, they donated their collection. I was not ever thinking maybe they would donate their collection someday, I was thinking I do not want to screw up their pronouns.

Barnard's flourishing zine community reflects the 15 years of hard work that Freedman has put into cultivating a robust collection of feminist and femme identity zines. In addition to students, she has seen an increased interest from faculty members in the zine collection, and continues outreach efforts to bring more classes and their professors into the library. In 2018 the Zine Library moved into a new building on campus that touts a Digital Humanities Center, and Freedman hopes that this will open up new ways in which researchers may use the collection. As the collection grows, Freedman curates the Barnard Zine Library to reflect inclusion and representation of people of all genders who are writing about feminism and femme identity. She remains committed to cataloging 14 zines a week, answering reference questions, and hosting international scholars traveling to work with the collection in person. Her drive to help women preserve and provide access to their stories has made available this unique cache of information to the world, and Barnard Zine Library will continue to promote the personal stories of often-marginalized writers.

Jenna Freedman is the Associate Director of Communications and Zine Librarian at Barnard Library & Academic Information Services. She holds a Master in Library and Information Science degree and hopes to earn another master's degree in Digital Humanities from the CUNY Graduate Center in December 2018. Her research focuses on zines and activist librarianship. Freedman is continually sought out for interviews, especially by aspiring library school students pursuing an interest in zine librarianship.

2.4.1 Takeaways

- Creating a DIY zine culture for women of color or any marginalized group can build a corpus of personal writings meant to be shared and distributed, and build a community of zine creators and readers.
- Providing access to non-traditional and alternative materials through cataloging them and making them part of the circulating collection enhances the reach and influence these writings have on the community and scholars.
- Inviting the community and/or campus to contribute to the development, engagement, and evolution of a transformative collection provides a sense of ownership and value to the collection.

2.5 Bellingham Alternative Library: with Cullen Beckhorn, Founder (Sept. 27, 2018)

519 E Maple St, Bellingham, WA 98225; http://altlib.org/; info@altlib.org

In 2007, artist and musician Cullen Beckhorn started Bellingham Alternative Library (hereafter referred to as AltLib) in the living room of a friend's Bellingham, Washington apartment where he had been couch surfing. Twenty years old at the time, Beckhorn was unsatisfied with the level of access to art education available to people in the city. Involved with the Students for a Democratic Society, he also noticed that there was no real centralizing hub in Bellingham for people interested in social change, activism, and direct action. Being interested in how spaces like record shops and bookstores have the potential to become locations for radical communities, Beckhorn decided that he would create a resource to fill this need. The result is an alternative library that presents the most recent, socially conscious thought through its collection, while at the same time serving as something akin to a community center.

Beginning with just a shelf's worth of books devoted largely to art, AltLib eventually outgrew the confines of the living room it started in and was subsequently relocated to a retail store space. In 2016, the library moved again—this time to 519 East Maple Street, a historic church build-ing on the edge of the campus of Western Washington University. Over the past 11 years of its operation, the library has grown from that single shelf of books to a collection of over 9000 items that, in addition to volumes on art, focuses on a variety of topics including radical subcultures and small press literature. What began as essentially a solo hobby project, AltLib is now a registered non-profit organization overseen by a board of directors and operated by a number of dedicated volunteers.

The library is a collective owned and run by its members, and operates in a manner similar to a food cooperative with people buying lifetime memberships (for projects with similar subscription models, see Estelita's Library, p. 38, and the Conscious Kid, p. 25). Lifetime memberships are $100 each, but members may pay incrementally over time, even as they continue to use the library and its resources. As members of the collective, people have certain voting rights including the power to vote on which books the library selects for its collection. In a novel arrangement that awards member participation, AltLib uses an algorithm on their website that determines what sort of voting power members have, assigning how much weight people have based on factors like the length of time that they have been involved with the library and how much feedback they have given about the collection.

AltLib attracts a wide variety of people from across Bellingham. In addition to the stacks of books, a big reason that people gravitate to the library is its role as a community hub. The library serves up a diverse menu of programming and services to its patrons (one is not required to obtain a membership for entry into the library, just to check out books, vote, and reserve meeting space). Programming includes special events like evening music concerts, theater, and poetry nights. Beckhorn is a free jazz musician and he hosts a lot of jazz and experimental music as well as local rock bands and other types of music. AltLib, he said, is "a social space and a place where people come to party, and I mean party in a wholesome way." The building also has a classroom that members may reserve for events, with recent calendar events including a weekly *Bhagavad Gita* reading group, International Workers of the World union meetings, and a workshop on rain/greywater harvesting. There is even an in-house bookstore that sells small press books, zines, records, and tapes, many of which are made by members of the local community. Finally, as is often the case with open community spaces, AltLib is a free space out of the weather that attracts people looking for a safe place. Beckhorn said "we are a little off the beaten path. We are up a hill so people have to put in the extra effort to climb the mountain, but it is a large thing that draws people into the space, people just looking for shelter or a place to be." While everyone is welcome at AltLib, Beckhorn noted that he was least prepared for this aspect of the library and that many library volunteers are unprepared to work with people with mental disabilities or with addiction. However, despite such challenges, one is struck by how organically the library fits within the community it serves, and how it is an active expression of that community.

Beckhorn manages the library's day-to-day operations, coordinating volunteers and working with various AltLib committees to keep things running smoothly. Besides himself, the library runs entirely on the contributions of its volunteer workers. There are four regular volunteer staff members that make sure that the space is open through the normal hours, as well as multiple volunteers that come and go as needed. Although the Western Washington University community is a source of many of the library's volunteers, Beckhorn said that AltLib's users consist of all types of people, folks whom are

> [...] interested and excited about doing something. I think of this place as a forum. It is for you to do whatever you want with it. That is how I pitch it to all people who are prospective volunteers. [...] Whatever you care about, you can bring that into the space. A volunteer coined a phrase for it, the "oligarchy of the interested." Basically, if you give a shit then your cares are going to be

*reflected through the shape that the space takes. I think one of the tenets that
we say we are founded on is volunteerism, which is just to say: if you are here
and putting the time in, it is going to serve you.*

This enthusiastic group of volunteers remains one of AltLib's major
strengths. Beckhorn warned that exhaustion is a potential challenge that
activists and organizers need to be prepared for, and, having learned from
experience, he cautioned against trying to take on too much work on
one's own:

*I mean, realistically, individual burnout is the biggest obstacle, feeling like "holy
shit, this is so much to take on." I would say if I were to start [AltLib] again, I
would put way more energy into trying to build a core group of people to
begin it rather than just going it solo for years and seeing who glommed onto
it. Yeah, definitely find people to share the work with and brainstorm with. As
that [collaboration] has become more a part of the space, it has allowed it to
grow so much more and just better serve the community.*

Having already undergone phenomenal growth and transformation
since its humble beginnings, AltLib continues to flourish, and it does so
with an eye trained strategically on the future. As a possible model for
expansion, Beckhorn looks to aspirational peers such as Providence,
Rhode Island's AS220 (http://as220.org), a non-profit arts institution
and printmaking cooperative that supports the local community. Like
AS220, he sees AltLib expanding to own numerous buildings around
town that all exist to support the arts in different ways. Acquiring ownership will allow AltLib to maintain maximum control over the collective's
own spaces. This, in turn, will allow the organization to get the most use
out of those spaces. Beckhorn said that such careful expansion would let
the library continue to develop other projects because "there is no shortage of cool things that could happen. It is a matter of funding and availability of space to make those things happen." Berkeley, California's
Slingshot Collective (https://slingshotcollective.org) is another inspiration
for Beckhorn and points to possibilities for AltLib's future; he sees
Slingshot as an example of how radical organizations have been able to
achieve self-sufficiency:

*[The Slingshot Collective] do a quarterly newspaper that is free that they
send out to radical spaces all over the world. The whole thing is funded by a
planner—like an organizer that they put together each year—and they send
a ton of copies to food coopts and info-shops all over the country and world
[. . .] And then the sales of that organizer fund pretty much their entire
project.*

AltLib has, in fact, recently written a grant to start a printmaking collective project that will occupy space at 519 East Maple Street. This project may afford them similar opportunities for growth and independence.

Finally, it is interesting to note that Beckhorn cites Lao Tzu's *Tao te Ching* as a major inspiration for the work that he does at AltLib. This connection is not surprising considering that work's profound themes of transformation, diversity, and unity, terms that have come to define what Beckhorn sees as Bellingham's "mix between an infoshop, community center, event space, bookstore, and library."

Cullen Beckhorn is a radical librarian, publisher, curator, musician, performance artist, utopian, and urban taoist based primarily in the unincorporated Cascadia bioregion. They are perhaps best known as the founder of the Alternative Library, and have worked extensively in other collaborative organizations since 2006. Cullen is the Director of Neoglyphic Media, which has produced publications, festivals, and artist projects since 2012.

2.5.1 Takeaways

- Consider alternative means of organization and operation. Why not create an "oligarchy of the interested?"
- Owning spaces like buildings will allow for maximum control over an organization's own spaces.
- Finding like-minded people to share work with may save you from potential burnout.

2.6 The Conscious Kid: with Ramon Stephens, Director (Oct. 5, 2018)

https://www.theconsciouskid.org/; consciouskidlibrary@gmail.com
California-based The Conscious Kid is a multifaceted critical media literacy organization and subscription lending library started by Ramon Stephens and his wife Katie Ishizuka after having difficulty finding books for their children that included Black characters:

I am Black, [Ishizuka is] Japanese. We could not find any, really any, books with Black characters. We found a few with some Asian characters, but for the most part, we were not finding much. We went to the public library and asked for a list of any and all Black [children's] books that they had. They only had really three books, and two of them were... Well, one was with a girl whose mom was praying to God that her hair would not be so nappy, and the other one was with this kid who had a bunch of animals living in her afro. Those are not the types of narratives we want to expose our kids to.

Stephens and Ishizuka noticed that there was not only a gap in the books offered representing underrepresented and marginalized groups, but even that those books that they did find in existing collections were largely not authored by people coming from the communities represented in the books. As a result, the two started collecting books by, for, and about marginalized groups. In the process of gathering this material, Stephens and Ishizuka started encountering and talking with parents and caregivers who were dealing with the same issues. They decided to transform their growing collection into a project to address this issue, and The Conscious Kid was born.

The Conscious Kid's lending library collection currently has close to 3000 books. The books are purchased by the organization itself or are received as donations from partner organizations or like-minded researchers and activists. The items cover a variety of intersectional themes including race, LGBTQIA + (lesbian, gay, bisexual, transgender, pansexual, genderqueer, queer, intersex, agender, asexual, and ally), gender, disability, immigration, and class, and they are selected for inclusion by means of a careful curation process which includes a consideration of how the characters are represented in the books, how characters relate to dominant groups, who wrote the book, who published the book, and what communities benefit and profit from the stories. While The Conscious Kid includes the work of mainstream authors in the collection, the organization tries to highlight independent authors:

It is actually really hard to find those books [that are best for the collection] from a lot of major publishers, and when you do the research on the publishing side you will find that they do not publish a lot of those books, and the ones they do are often not authored by in-group members, or contain problematic or stereotypical depictions of marginalized groups. So our collection does consist of a lot of independent authors. We are proud of being able to provide a platform for some of these authors that have not had access to mainstream publishing support.

Subscribers sign up for three, six, or twelve months at a time at approximately 10 dollars a month. When joining the program, new members identify the types of materials that they are looking to provide their young readers. So, for example, if subscribers want books that provide diverse gender representation, or they want things that deal with positive depictions of Black males, The Conscious Kid uses this information to curate to the individual subscriber's needs while at the same time developing the lending library. Members then get three books mailed to them every month that fit their chosen categories and simply return the books when finished. There is also a purchase option, so if people want to be sent books they can keep; they can sign up for the book-of-the-month option. Coordinating all of this is a time-intensive, complex process. Book packages must be sent out every month to the 100—150 regular subscribers, requiring the selection, packaging, and shipping of the books.

In addition to curating and delivering the books, Stephens and Ishizuka—the two run most of the daily operations of The Conscious Kid—spend a large portion of their time scouring the literature for timely information related to equity and anti-oppression to post to their social media sites on Twitter, Facebook, and Instagram. They aim to publish one to three social media posts a day that discuss important authors, social justice work being done, related issues in the community, and/or useful tools and resources for parents, caregivers, and educators. Finding fresh content for their blog and social media outlets can be challenging. Stephens noted that a common practice for many social justice organizations is to repost what other have already put online. However, while reposting is effective for creating solidarity, there are instances, he said, when certain voices are ignored or might receive less space. The Conscious Kid tries to identify and fill these gaps. This is important but oftentimes grueling work.

The Conscious Kid also provides training workshops for educators in a variety of different contexts such as high schools or colleges. Workshops focus on critical media literacy and children's books, these books' representation of dominant and non-dominant groups, and the selection of material for young readers. In addition to preparing for these events, the workshops involve a lot of traveling. So far, travel has mostly been limited to Southern California, but they have had previous and current projects reach beyond the state.

In addition to all of this, The Conscious Kid actively produces its own original research focusing on the critical media analysis of children's literature. One recent study (Ishizuka & Stephens, 2019), published in *Research on Diversity in Youth Literature*, is a critical analysis of Dr. Seuss's (Theodor Geisel) children's books and contends with recurring themes of non-inclusivity such as anti-Blackness, Orientalism, and white supremacy.

When queried about how The Conscious Kid has been able to accomplish so much over a short time, Stephens identified three challenges faced over their first years of operation: (1) team-building, (2) fundraising, and, (3) dealing with white fragility and racism from people opposed to The Conscious Kid's work. How The Conscious Kid faced these challenges may prove to be instructive to anyone considering similar work.

Building an effective team can mean the difference between success and burnout. Stephens said that while it is possible to do social justice work by oneself, working alone can be stressful. It is important to find other people to not only absorb some of the labor, but also to motivate you and provide resilience. The Conscious Kid team currently consists of five people, and everyone brings their unique perspective to the organization allowing team members to leverage each other's individual strengths. Stephens and Ishizuka are both extensively trained in social justice and advocacy work. One of the other team member specializes in understanding the interstices of Latinx identity, gender, and social work. Another brings a knowledge in the experiences of marginalized religious groups, as well as provides professional advice on navigating the educational system.

Fundraising is a challenge reported repeatedly by the organizations profiled in this book, and The Conscious Kid is particularly familiar with this obstacle. The organization's money for buying books is limited, so "trying to get as much money as we can to buy these books is difficult, but it is more than that. It is [also challenging] to motivate people to see that these issues may actually be important."

Cultivating partners and allies is of equal importance. Stephens said that one way to make things happen is to look to other people that are doing similar work and to figure out how to reach out and build partnerships:

There is not usually a lot of money, so you have to learn how to leverage other people in the field. Everybody that does this work kind of knows one another because it is a limited field, but [the small community] really is helpful because you can start to share platforms and share resources. Building your network out is another important part.

Attesting to their own networking skill, The Conscious Kid has initiated partnerships with organizations outside of California such as the Brooklyn Children's Museum and Baton Rouge's Line 4 Line Barbershop.

A third, and particularly unfortunate, obstacle that The Conscious Kid has encountered is explicit racism and hostile attacks from those who misunderstand what they are doing with the organization. Such obnoxious push back, Stephens said, is an ongoing problem: "We have people who have threatened us. We have people that write us emails saying that we should be shot, you name it. It is every single week that we get threats come in." Learning to navigate controversy, hostile environments, and potentially hateful attacks, therefore, is an important tool for maintaining an activist's personal mental health. Once again, the value of team building asserts itself here, and "having my team there to provide that mental health support," Stephens said, "is a really important part of the process."

The fact that all of this important work has been done by a small organization starting out with limited resources demonstrates how a few dedicated activists working together may accomplish big tasks.

Ramon Stephens founded The Conscious Kid with Katie Ishizuka in 2016. Ramon currently holds a B.A. in political science and comparative history, a master's in Education, and is working towards a Ph.D in education.

Katie Ishizuka holds a B.A in business and a master's in macro Social Work.

2.6.1 Takeaways

- It is possible to effectively address a particular issue—in this instance, we saw critical media literacy—in various ways at the same time.
- Reposting others' work is effective for creating solidarity, but there are instances when certain voices are ignored or might receive less space. Actively seek to identify and close these gaps.
- Small organizations can be successful if they carefully build teams and partnerships.
- Be prepared for conflict and rely upon team members and other allies for support.

2.7 Durland Alternatives Library: with Ryan Clover-Owens, Director (Sept. 10, 2018)

130 Anabel Taylor Hall, Cornell University, Ithaca, NY 14853, 607-255-6486; https://www.alternativeslibrary.org/

Founded in 1973 by Lewis H. and Margaret C. Durland as a way to celebrate the life of their late daughter Anne Carry Durland (St. Lifer & Rogers, 1994), Durland Alternatives Library (DAL) houses a unique collection of alternative materials commemorating Anne's deep concern for community and ecology (Andersen, 2012, p. 64). Located on the Cornell University campus and affiliated with the non-profit organization Center for Transformative Action (http://www.centerfortransformativeaction. org/), the DAL collection contains about 10,000 items including "books, alternative press periodicals, audio and video materials on natural healing, alternative education, human rights, renewable energy, and multicultural studies, among other subjects" (St. Lifer & Rogers, 1994, p. 25). As a radical library, DAL continues to curate materials on social justice, ecology, and transformative action (Durland Alternatives Library, 2018), serving underrepresented and marginalized groups by preserving the integrity of the collection and providing them with access to its materials to help address environmental, societal, and political issues.

People often see libraries as community institutions that support citizens' interaction with political and civic issues through offering spaces and resources to facilitate exchange of dialogue (Jaeger, Taylor, & Gorham, 2015). A large part of DAL programming centers on its core mission to provide access to challenging, transformative, even unorthodox materials. For example, the DAL Shaleshock Media Archive Project collects video footage of hydraulic fracking activity captured by local videographers, records pertaining to town board meetings and public forums on the issue, and interviews conducted with environmental activists over a five-year period.

DAL helps patrons on the Cornell University campus as well as the wider public through its collaboration with the Finger Lakes Library System, a cooperative library system serving 33 public libraries located in Ithaca, New York and surrounding counties. DAL uses its inter-library loan system and other Web-based infrastructure to provide access beyond the campus, and Lynn Anderson, former DAL Director, reached out to the Finger Lakes System to integrate its circulating collection into the system's online catalog. On an average day, DAL sees researchers, students, and community users accessing their collection. The place is popular, with many patrons returning repeatedly. Current DAL Director Ryan Clover-Owens said, "During the school year and when there are events on campus, we have quite a following of patrons that say, 'I have been coming here for 30 years' or 'I grew up coming to this library.'" Before becoming

Director, Clover-Owens, was himself a longtime patron of the library, spending his teenage years at the library listening to recorded alternative radio programs that interviewed activists and authors. Such loyalty is not surprising when one considers the effort that DAL puts into supporting the evolving needs of their patrons and making them feel welcomed, and many people use this space for collaborative activities and social engagements. It has incorporated a small café, as well as a lighted stage for special events, and the book stacks are on wheels and moveable to create spaces for student use for events such as campus club meetings. In addition to providing community spaces and library resources, outreach and programming is a major part of daily activities at DAL, keeping it visible to patrons and integrating it into their lives.

One exciting DAL program is the Cornell Lending Library (CLL), which provides needed assistance to first-generation college students. Cornell's first-generation students come from various socioeconomic backgrounds, and many cannot afford expensive textbooks and other required reading materials on top of steep tuition costs. In order to break down barriers to information access, a group of students started the textbook lending program on campus, at first operating out of dorm rooms. Clover-Owens said that the students were "kind-of baffled that they could not get any institutional support for [their grassroots lending library]." Eventually they asked DAL to host their program, and the library, in collaboration with Cornell's First-in-Class initiative, now assists CLL by facilitating free, semester long loans of textbooks to first generation students, offering shelving space, managing the CLL's cataloging, book repairs, and circulation notifications (Cornell University Library, 2018).

DAL programs also reach far beyond campus, and the library is home to the successful Prisoner Express program (http://prisonerexpress.org). Fifteen years ago, Prisoner Express Program Director Gary Fine was inspired to start the initiative when an incarcerated person requested materials from DAL via traditional mail. Fine began "answering the letters and sending out boxes of books... [and] by the end of six months, we were getting a dozen letters a week" (Andersen, 2003, p. 62). After realizing that DAL could meet these requests, even more prisoners started to write-in and request books. Since then, the program has grown to over 4000 active participants with approximately 15,000 participant names in its database and hundreds of request for books coming in every day. Cornell work-study students open letters, sort, and code them before writing the prisoners back with direct personal responses.

Prisoner Express not only provides prisoners with library resources and materials, but also facilitates a creative exchange program with prisoners in which the latter share their poetry, personal essays, and transformative experiences with one another. There is also a DAL sponsored art show that displays prisoner work alongside the work of political artists. Through these programs, the library has developed a way for a marginalized population to tell their stories and share their experiences, bring themselves together as a community, and support "a transformation of the shared story to one of hope, resilience, and opportunity for change. Not only is mutual aid a relief for many to find they are not alone; it can be a source of social transformation and energy for change" (Erickson, 2018, p. 133).

Clover-Owens told us that "on the edges, [there are] things that are not mainstream, but are actively facing and confronting problems in our society." In college, he read David Abram's (1997) classic work on natural philosophy and human ecology, *Spell of the sensuous*. Abram's point, Clover-Owens said,

> Is that there has always been this valuable role of the person who lived on the edge, in the edges, of the community. Their job... even if they are scaring people... they remind people that things are mysterious. We just cannot control everything and cannot live on our assumptions. We always have to be curious about what is on the other side and be open to receiving that instead of just being afraid of it or afraid of new things.

Breaking down barriers to access and advocating for marginalized groups, whether on campus, in Ithaca and surrounding counties, or outside these borders, will always be part of the advocacy and activism fueling DAL. The organization sees itself as being accountable to the people who support what they do. Clover-Owens sees the organization as a "proactive media organization" and the library's journey as a continual process of adapting and tailoring the library to its patrons. He anticipates that DAL's next big shift will be to blend the world of online media and social exchange with its unique collections. He wants the library to spark curiosity and possibility beyond the building to support people who desire to transform the world in a time of political and social upheaval. He envisions that providing more discoverability and access to materials through modern social media will continue to advance the library's objective to stimulate solutions to seemingly insurmountable problems.

Before becoming Director of Durland Alternatives Library in 2012, Ryan Clover-Owens was inspired by the DIY ethic in the hip-hop and punk music communities and the idea of self-publishing and self-producing. Attending Antioch College in Ohio, Clover-Owens coordinated an environmental group whose headquarters were at the campus library, developing his appreciation for information work. In 2002, he started an extensive zine collection and later a small library, the DIY Resource Center, which offered workshops on self-publishing. His activist nature and drive to serve his community through making available alterative information resources made him an ideal candidate to direct DAL.

2.7.1 Takeaways

- Information workers must question the normative structures found in society and equip citizens with the materials and resources they need to change structures when they are found to be lacking.
- Supporting the evolving needs of patrons and making them feel welcomed inspires loyalty and support.
- Materials "on the edges" may be less mainstream and may appear to be of marginal importance, but they are essential artifacts that may one-day impact society.
- Marginalized communities deserve access to information resources as a basic human right.
- All libraries are potential incubators for creativity, possibility, and advocacy.

2.8 East Side Freedom Library: with Peter Rachleff, Co-Founder and Co-Executive Director (Aug. 28, 2018)

1105 Greenbrier Street, St. Paul, MN 55106; (651)-207-4926; https://eastsidefreedomlibrary.org/; info@eastsidefreedomlibrary.org

Saint Paul, Minnesota's East Side Freedom Library (ESFL) opened its doors to the public in 2014. Housed in a beautiful Beaux-Arts style Carnegie Library building in the culturally diverse Payne-Phalen neighborhood, ESFL's mission is "to inspire solidarity, advocate for justice and work toward equity for all" (East Side Freedom Library, n.d.-a). To support this objective, the library provides access to an impressive research collection of over 20,000 books and other media in a variety of collection categories such as "Labor and working-class history and literature,"

"Jazz and radical music history," "Asian American and Asian history," and "Women's history and feminism(s)" (East Side Freedom Library, n.d.-a). ESFL also houses the Hmong Archives, a 171,000 item collection documenting "the story of the Hmong community in Minneapolis and Saint Paul, Minnesota, as well as Hmong communities around the world" (Hmong Archives, n.d.). It also houses collections donated by important scholars, activists, and artists. Despite its impressive collections, the organization is much more than a cache of organized information for researching social justice and labor issues. It is a community focal point, providing a robust calendar of programming including concerts, film showings, discussion groups, and oral history projects.

We spoke with Peter Rachleff, the retired Macalester College history professor who cofounded ESFL with his partner Beth Cleary, who is currently a professor of Theater and Dance at Macalester. Rachleff has a long history of labor activism and social justice work that informs what he does at the library. A protégé of both famed council communist Paul Mattick Sr. and influential labor historian David Montgomery, Rachleff studied labor history at the University of Pittsburgh. He went on to teach college himself, educating people that would themselves become everything from union organizers, to community organizers, to professors. During these years he also became directly involved with the radical labor periodicals *Root and Branch* and *Labor Notes* magazine. In the 1980s, Rachleff was chairperson of the Twin Cities Support Committee for Local P-9 (which organized solidarity with the Hormel meatpacking strikers of 1985—86). In 2005—06, Rachleff played a similar role in support of striking Northwest Airlines mechanics. ESFL came largely as a response to Rachleff and Cleary's move in the late 1990s to Saint Paul's East Side, a neighborhood then (as it is now) in the midst of economic and demographic transitions, deindustrialization, and the loss of unionized jobs. A diverse and multicultural place, immigrants from Sweden, Ireland, Eastern Europe, Mexico, and, most recently, Southeast Asia, Africa, and Central America have all contributed to its richness. In light of this diversity, Rachleff and Cleary considered ways to build bridges between and among the communities that make up the East Side. Manhattan's Hatch-Billops Collection (https://www.nyc-arts.org/organizations/275/hatch-billops-collection) served as a major inspiration and model for ESFL:

> [James V. Hatch and Camille Billops] were very active in the Black art scene in New York, and they began to develop an archive in their living space. They had

bought a loft in a building in SoHo in Chinatown and Lower Manhattan at the time when such space was cheap, and they began to build a collection and to supplement their archives by doing oral history interviews with people of color. They also produced an annual journal called Artist and Influence *which published for 30 years, and they did a cable access television show of interviews done in front of salon audiences that would morph into broader discussions. When we met them in the late 1990s Beth [Cleary] was directing two plays that had been anthologized in a book that Jim Hatch had edited. I went to meet them to get Jim's permission to use the script, and we fell in love with the work that they were doing there. So, as we were confronting the way our neighborhood around us was changing, we were thinking of how these two people had brought different skill sets into collaboration with each other, had created a space that honored history, and a space that sought to tell the stories that often were not told.*

Rachleff and Cleary returned to Minnesota with the germ of an idea to start something similar to Hatch-Billops. Rachleff's own academic research also informed the idea behind ESFL. In the 1980s he had done research at the University of Minnesota's Immigration History Research Center. During the process, Rachleff met many fascinating fellow researchers and learned from them a great deal of what would become important to him about his own research interests. This dialogue, he said, encouraged him to think about how to create a space where people would want to interact with each other while reading or doing research. ESFL would become such a space.

Searching for a location to house their new 501c3 non-profit organization, Rachleff and Cleary learned that the city was about to abandon the Arlington Hills Branch of the Saint Paul Public Library housed in the East Side neighborhood's historic Carnegie library. Rachleff said that the building was an ideal location for a cultural center and library, having a lot of social meaning as well as a good vibe. Although the building had a steep price tag on its outright purchase, successful negotiations led to an agreement with the city on a long-term lease, and ESFL opened its doors just months after the Arlington Hills Branch moved out. In five years, ESFL has gained the financial support of 1300 individuals and more than 20 unions. It has built a mailing list of more than 5000 addresses, and has become a popular venue for all sorts of activities, from theater and music to author talks and panel discussions.

The library's profile has increased dramatically, and this gain comes largely as a result of the co-founders' concerted efforts to understand the communities that they serve and to make the ESFL part of those communities:

> One of the first things that we did was get a grant to commission a Hmong visual artist to paint a mural down the stairwell of the building. We brought focus groups from different communities beginning with Native Americans, Swedes, Italians, Germans, African-Americans, Latinos, Hmong, and Karen. They told him stories, and he created this amazing mural of East Side stories. We wanted the mural to say to people when they walk in the door, "here are your stories right here on the wall. Your stories exist in history and are honored in this space."

Furthermore, ESFL has engaged in extensive community outreach efforts to achieve community buy-in, holding neighborhood events like outdoor music concerts and barbecues. They are also in the process of getting more of their ESFL produced literature translated into languages other than English, so even if a program or event is not offered in a particular language spoken in the neighborhood, people know that the library is making an effort to reach them in ways that are comfortable to them.

Rachleff explained that there are no typical days at ESFL. While some days may be slow with only a few readers using the collections, other days find the place a beehive of activity that demonstrate ESFL's organic connection with the East Side and beyond:

> Today is a relatively quiet day here. Tomorrow though... Every Wednesday there is a group of Karen (from Burma/Myanmar) women who come from 9:30 am until about 3:00 pm. They bring portable backstrap looms. We have an open room downstairs with a frame, and they hook up to the frame. This summer they have not only been here themselves on Wednesdays, they also come in on Thursdays and Fridays to teach Hmong teenagers how to weave. While that is going on tomorrow, downstairs the hotel and restaurant workers union in town will have a daylong organizer where they are working with college students to try to unionize the food service departments at the various private colleges in Saint Paul and Minneapolis. Late in the day, there will be a cohort of student services' staff from University of Wisconsin River Falls coming to learn about the immigrant history of this neighborhood.

Since there is only one paid staff member and volunteers essentially run the library, Rachleff advised that the best way to manage a successful enterprise in such a vibrant environment is to determine what people are willing to give, and to accept that contribution graciously. Different people have different amounts of time and money, and they may have different focuses and interests. A project as big as ESFL, which includes "everything from cleaning the bathrooms to raising money for the heating and cooling system, to cataloging books, to interacting with people who walk in off the street...," requires that social justice organizers and activists identify people's particular passions and skills, as well as their inclination to offer those passions and skills in service of the organization:

> I think that rather than saying we need A, B, and C, and then going out to find people that will give us A, B, and C, the task is to find out what people are willing and able to give, and to try to create the opportunity for them to give it and be appreciated for that. Cumulatively, it is remarkable what happens when you do that.

The work that ESFL is doing today is as timely and vital as it has ever been. The current political situation in the United States has manifested in what Rachleff described as "a sense of immediacy." For instance, a lot of the work currently done at the library involves labor unions. Many people expect the recent Supreme Court decision concerning government workers and collective bargaining to hurt union funding and, as a result, this has bolstered a wave of local labor activism that makes good use of ESFL, both for its trove of relevant information and for its capacity to facilitate dialogue, build community, and develop class-consciousness. Rachleff said that today's political milieu shows that now is an important time for critical thinking, and that "we have to figure out where we go from here, so the production of critical ideas is more important now than ever. It gets too easy to just say that [Donald Trump] is a buffoon and we should impeach him." The library has become a ground for engaging in this type of thought, as well as an intersection where activism and scholarship meet—a site that fosters radical praxis.

ESFL celebrated its fifth anniversary in summer 2019, and its future looks bright. Over 120 people attended the anniversary event that featured a presentation on "The Half Life of Freedom" by author, activist, and *New Yorker* magazine contributor Jelani Cobb (East Side Freedom Library, 2019-b). The library has also recently published a history of the ESFL and the neighborhood that it serves, *Reinventing the People's Library* (Gaut, 2019).

Peter Rachleff (*he/him/his*) is an historian by training and trade and a social justice activist from the core of his being. From 1982–2012 he taught labor, immigration, and African American history at Macalester College in St. Paul, Minnesota, and in 2014, he and Beth Cleary co-founded the East Side Freedom Library (https://eastsidefreedomlibrary.org)

with the mission to "inspire solidarity, advocate for justice, and work toward equity for all."

2.8.1 Takeaways

- Make an effort to reach your community and/or patrons in ways that are comfortable to them. Know your community. Walk your neighborhood.
- When asking for help with your organization, particularly volunteer help, find out what people are willing to give, and graciously accept what they offer.
- The production of critical ideas is crucial in today's political environment. One should design transformative information spaces in ways to foster this kind of work.

2.9 Estelita's Library: with Edwin Lindo, Owner (Sept. 21, 2018)

2533 16th Ave S. Seattle, WA; (415)-342-9009; http://estelitaslibrary.com; estelitaslibrary@gmail.com

Started in May 2018, Seattle, Washington's Estelita's Library (hereafter referred to as "Estelita's") is a community social justice lending library operating on a membership model. Estelita's also serves food, beer, and wine, has regular programming and events, and acts as a community meeting point and cultural center.

No stranger to social activism and community organizing, Estelita's proprietor Edwin Lindo had fought against police brutality in the San Francisco area, opposed gentrification in the city's neighborhoods, and worked for equality of education for students of color. After moving to Seattle, he opened up Estelita's using mostly his personal collection of social justice related material, with additional books coming later as donations. Lindo had benefitted greatly from the knowledge in his collection and wanted to share it with others. He said that he sought out "a way to decentralize the knowledge from these books and give folks more access to them." Seeing that there was a space opening up across the street from a local Seattle coffee shop that he frequented, Lindo asked the owner of the building if he would be open to him starting up a community library there. The building's owner said yes, and the library, named after Lindo's daughter Estella, quickly became a fixture in the neighborhood.

Estelita's is a purposively small operation that is open from three to 8 p.m. Tuesday through Friday and twelve to 5 p.m. on the weekends. For inspiration, Lindo looked to Radio Habana Social Club, a popular Cuban restaurant in San Francisco's Mission District that is cozy and packed with beautiful art. Membership libraries, i.e., organizations where subscribers pay a monthly or yearly fee to gain access to the collection (see Conscious Kid, p. 25, for another example), have a long history in the US. Lindo himself fondly remembered using the Mechanic's Institute Library & Chess Room, a membership library in San Francisco, when he was a child. Estelita's, however, is unique in that it focuses nearly exclusively on social justice issues. There is no previous model of a membership library, Lindo said, "where it is a social justice library that actually has books in circulation, that also has programing, and that serves food and wine. [Estelita's] is more of a community hub that can cultivate culture." The membership model works on a sliding scale of 30–50 dollars a year. Once people become members, they receive a membership card and are then able to check out any of the books in the collection. When we interviewed Lindo, Estelita's had been in operation for only three-and-a-half months and was already doing well with a membership base of over 250 people. Most of the library's members are from the Seattle area, but there are some who live as far away as Vancouver, British Columbia. Remarkably, approximately 20% of members live outside of Seattle (distance members return loaned books by mail if they cannot make it back to the library in person). The library's membership is also notable for its diversity, and Lindo said that he has observed people of every economic group and racial makeup visit the library.

The 2000 item collection is solidly focused on social justice issues and related topics. Estelita's interprets social justice broadly, offering books on political theory, radical political theory, race, gender and sexual identity, liberation struggles, and the historical experiences of oppressed peoples. Besides the non-fiction selections, there are fiction books written by authors of color and novels that speak to the particular experiences of oppressed peoples. There is also a popular collection of children's books that focuses on liberation struggles and the counter-narrative history of the material found in traditional history lessons. Finally, there are about 20 books falling into the area of what Lindo referred to as related to "Colonizer Studies." These items include traditional "American History" books so that readers may explore how American history as an academic institution has created its own dominant historical narrative—one that represents the viewpoint of the oppressor. While all of the books are cataloged, no categories have been assigned for physically ordering the books on the shelves, nor does Estelita's employ a classification system like Dewey Decimal Classification. This casual approach to organization allows for reader serendipity when browsing the shelves. Lindo explained that there is also a lack of classificatory and categorical strictures for philosophical reasons:

> I see the problematic structure of the ordering systems, particularly the Dewey Decimal System where its intention was to support academics and their ability to find a particular book. What I actually intended was to support community members who came in and said that they would like to learn more. The other part is that commercial bookstores have a "Black History," or have an "American History," or a "German Studies" section. You may have an interest, and you may go to a section, but [the categorization] often excludes you from being able to explore something else that is actually very much related. You won't see it because the struggle of Black folks in Germany will be in the "German Studies," but not "Black History."

Lindo's heterodox approach to library organization explodes the rigid controls found in traditionally hierarchical organizations such as those used in academic libraries and government funded public libraries. He said that he often looks to the work of Brazilian philosopher of education, Paolo Freire, for inspiration. Freire's pedagogical ideas subvert dominant, hierarchical modes of education (and hence social control) by blurring the line between student and teacher. Lindo said "I think fundamentally [Freire's] approach to both education and how we deal with systems of oppression are necessary to understand, and I think it would be helpful if we actually embrace his approach to knowledge and structural oppression." Estelita's, as a result, essentially becomes a tool for achieving what Freire (2018) referred to as conscientzao (consciousness raising). It is a space where everyone contributes to the learning of others, where people become conscious of what is going on in society without slipping into prescribed roles or being restricted to predetermined—as well as artificial—categories and social structures. Providing an example of the liberation that such an environment offers, Lindo said that

> What has happened is that there have been a lot of Black, brown, and queer folks that are pursuing either PhD's or master's degrees, and they have been coming to the library and saying: "Finally, I have a place where I can be myself

and be an academic and not be judged on what I do, or where I am, or any-thing. I can just be me."

In addition to the collection, Estelita's Library provides a place for programming for and by the community, offering events such as spoken word nights and book talks. For example, Naomi Klein's (2007) *Shock doctrine: The rise of disaster capitalism* was the subject of one recent talk. Lindo said that the programming does not come from him, but from the community: "It is the community that says 'this is something we want to do, can we use the space?' What that does is facilitate ownership by the community." It is this focus on community building, and the sense of empowerment and agency that it engenders, that sets Estelita's apart from many bookstores and public libraries, that makes it a counter-hegemonic effort. It transcends being a "service" in the manner of a bookstore or public library, becoming an organic part of the community and a community investment. For example, while Lindo pays the rent, the community helps immensely with the space, making it a truly shared resource. When he made it known he wanted to open up the library, local community members volunteered to help out, for instance offering to help him shelve all of the books. It got to the point, Lindo said:

> where people were continually coming to the library, and they said, "you know, if you cannot make it one day or if you do not happen to be able to open on time, let me know and I will open for you." We do not have a volunteer system, or coordinator, or any of that, but people in the community have just stepped up and said "We want to keep these doors open, even if it means me doing it." We are so blessed for that because there are days I just cannot get there by the time we open; and on the back end, there are people there who want to stay and read [after closing time], and I say "I am going to go to my family. This is your home. You just have to close the lower lock and close the door on the way out." We let them make it their space and, and it is their community home.

The basic motivation behind Estelita's may be, initially at least, confusing to some people, especially because the intention behind its operation is not to make money. This mode of operation appears to fly in the face of conventional wisdom in the modern capitalist world. Lindo's goal, literally, is just to keep the door open. The real fruit of his labor is what the community makes from it. "My hope," Lindo said, "is that folks of color, and other oppressed folks, know this is a safe place."

Edwin Lindo, JD, is owner of Estelita's Library, a social justice membership library located in Seattle, Washington. When not at Estelita's,

Edwin works as a lecturer at the University of Washington, where he teaches courses on Race, Racism, Medicine, and Law.

2.9.1 Takeaways

- Size does not always matter. Small places and things can become community focal points, their intimate nature nurturing feelings of community ownership.
- Positive change may require doing away with traditional structures and conventions, even if some of these conventions, such as the Dewey Decimal System, may initially appear to be benign.
- When your project invests in the community, the community becomes invested in your project. The community and the project may become synonymous.

2.10 Interference Archive: with Kevin Caplicki, Co-Founder, and Bonnie Gordon, Volunteer Worker (Oct. 2, 2018)

314 7th St, Brooklyn, NY 11215; info@interferencearchive.org

Interference Archive (IA) is a volunteer run, Brooklyn-based collection of literature, audiovisual media, artifacts, and ephemera related to social movements, activism, and grassroots organizing efforts happening throughout the world. It is also a space providing "public programs including exhibitions, workshops, talks, and screenings, all of which encourage critical and creative engagement with the rich history of social movements" (Interference Archive, n.d.-a). Kevin Caplicki, Molly Fair, Dara Greenwald, and Josh MacPhee founded IA in the wake of *Signs of Change: Social Movement Cultures 1960s to Now*, a successful 2009 exhibition of social movement and protest related materials produced by artists MacPhee and Greenwald. Gathering materials for the exhibition, however, turned out to be somewhat difficult due to a lack of proper cataloging and/or a perception of the material's insignificance on the part of the holding institutions, which translated into inaccessibility. Caplicki, himself an artist and community organizer, told us that while the materials might not have been highly valued by the institutions that housed them—possibly because they were produced anonymously or by marginal groups with limited cultural or economic persuasion—MacPhee and Greenwald saw their historical significance and lasting cultural value. The experience prompted the two to begin gathering materials for what would develop into IA.

In 2011, Greenwald was diagnosed with cancer (she has since passed away), motivating the creation of a permanent space where the IA collection could be made available to the public, an information center for social movement and activist related materials overlooked and/or not normally desired by more traditional institutions. The four cofounders discussed the development of a public space where people might easily access this sort of material for usage and research. They secured a location in Brooklyn's Park Slope neighborhood, and IA opened to the public in December of that year.

Social movements produce many information artifacts meant for display in public spaces, and IA honors this idea by combining open access shelving with an exhibit area and space for related programming. The collection consists of variety of materials spanning over forty years, including stickers, buttons, posters, zines, serials, moving image materials, and audio formats (records and cassettes). Subject areas in the collection range from anarchism, activism, European squatter movements, and African American and Latin American liberation movements (Petrossiants, 2017). Every object in the archive is available for the patrons to explore, and users are encouraged to search on their own through the archival boxes and discover topics spontaneously (Gordon, Hanna, Hoyer, & Ordaz, 2016). The place curates three to four well-attended exhibits a year, and Bonnie Gordon, one of approximately 95 volunteer workers, said that such exhibits "activate" the materials in the community and "actively connects the [collection] to current social events." Gordon said that the accessibility to the materials is what drew her to the collection, and that the level of engagement with the collection is rewarding to everyone involved. Caplicki echoed this sentiment when he described IA as a locus for the active, dialogical creation of knowledge and societal transformation:

> The use of these objects is [the collection's] preservation and engagement with the objects is [the collection's] reproduction. [. . .] We want people to learn about social justice. We want to inspire them to struggle for social justice in a contemporary sense. We want people to know their history, but while they move forward in engaging with the world in more of a social justice way.

One example of this powerful generative dialogue in action is IA's graphic production workshops. As part of its programming and outreach to the community, the organization conducts "Propaganda Parties," i.e., workshops that provide community members the opportunity to learn screen-printing and to make their own activist materials. Some of these creations end up being widely distributed or become part of the IA collection itself, benefiting future users.

The archive's visitors run the gamut from local community members to students and researchers. IA also welcomes artists and activists with an interest in radical history. High school and college teachers bring their students for tours and presentations on how collection materials relate to their curriculum. The place even has a children's book area and hosts "Radical Playdates" for kids. One recent Playdate, for example, had young participants creating posters based on memorable quotes by activist, writer, and librarian Audre Lorde. Caplicki described what happens when people come to IA:

We [now] have a store front, where for six years we were in a warehouse building, an old factory building, so [back then], it was much more of a destination for people that were familiar with the project, and they were coming to look for something specific. Now it is a mixture of people coming to see exhibitions, or they are coming to do research, so it is a matter of inviting them in and introducing them into the space, introducing them to how we have things organized, and that we have all of our materials [available through] open stacks.

Although large swathes of the collection still await cataloging, IA is a browsing archive. Patrons are encouraged to peruse the finding aids, and the staff help them retrieve the appropriate boxes on the topics they are researching. Caplicki uses his deep knowledge of the collection to help visitors find materials that would benefit their research. Although he does not know every piece in the collection, he often aids patrons with exploratory searches that uncover intriguing materials and hidden treasures.

IA organizes itself non-hierarchically. There are seven working groups—Administration, Cataloging, Born Digital, Audio Archive, Education, Exhibitions, and Staffing—that divide up responsibilities and function through the efforts of many volunteers (Interference Archive, n.d.-b). Even so, with so much happening at IA, the lack of sufficient people power to keep up with things remains a pressing limitation. The organization, therefore, prioritizes events based on the availability of space and the level of community participation, so IA chooses to focus primarily on events that welcome the public and members of the activist and artist communities. Perhaps IA's largest challenge is the exorbitant cost of rent, with about three-quarters of the organization's budget going towards rent and utilities. Donations through community fundraising keeps the doors open, and most of these donations come from individuals—whom Gordon refers to as "people sustainers"—who contribute from ten to fifty dollars per month. IA also receive small grants, which it uses for exhibits and programming.

There are big plans for the future. The organization is working on purchasing a digitization station to allow patrons to digitize their own materials as well as items from the collection, and they hope to install viewing stations that will give visitors more options for accessing media. Although IA presently loans out items for exhibits, one long-term goal is to operate their own touring exhibit. Regardless of such individual projects, Caplicki and Gordon agreed that collecting and programming related to grassroots organizing and progressive social movements must remain foundational elements of the archive. They imagine that the collection, which has already doubled in size since 2011, will continue to grow in support of these themes. It also remains of paramount importance that IA thrives as a public space, maintains a high level of community involvement, and remains a resource and outlet for artists and activists.

Kevin Caplicki is an artist, organizer, farmer, and one contributor to the materials that Interference Archive houses. Before cofounding IA, Caplicki worked in radical bookstores and info-shops, and he collected ephemera produced by international movements and active campaigns. He credits Josh MacPhee as having an incredible influence on him as a mentor, helping to cultivate his knowledge, and introducing him to social movement histories.

Bonnie Gordon received a master's in Archives and Public History from New York University (NYU) in the spring of 2014. While completing her degree, Gordon worked as a graduate student assistant at NYU's Tamiment Library and Robert F. Wagner Labor Archives. She started volunteering at Interference Archive while in graduate school, and has continued to do so even while working full time as a Digital Archivist. At IA, Gordon is a member of the Administration, Cataloging, and Born Digital Working Groups, and occasionally helps with staffing and exhibits.

2.10.1 Takeaways

- Social justice movements produce materials meant to be accessible and utilized, and it is the responsibility of transformative library and information projects to tend to their preservation and accessibility when traditional organizations may remain apathetic.

- Volunteer-based projects promote use and buy-in from the surrounding community.
- Open stack archives allow patrons to explore and discover unique materials, making them counter-hegemonic.

2.11 Provisions Library: with Donald Russell, Co-Founder and Executive Director (Sept. 24, 2018)

Provisions Research Center for Arts & Social Change, George Mason University, 4400 University Dr, Fairfax, VA 22030; (202)-670-7768

Provisions Library (PL) is the creation of Gaylord Neely, President of the philanthropic grant making organization Gaea Foundation (http://www.gaeafoundation.org/Gaea.html), and art curator and present PL Executive Director Donald Russell. PL was initially funded in 2001 by the Gaea Foundation through a five-year seed grant, over which time the project worked "to bring about social change by identifying and amplifying compelling voices of thinkers, writers, and artists from around the world" (Provisions Library, 2012a).

We interviewed Russell for this profile, who explained the origin and meaning of the project's moniker:

We spent many months sorting through names. Provisions emerged from a staff conversation when Gaylord Neely mentioned that the organization should be like a knapsack to take on a journey, and that led to what needs to be in a knapsack, namely provisions. We did a deep dive into the meaning of the word, and we appreciated the connotation of provisional, i.e., existing only when needed. Finally, we really loved the way it also means Pro (in favor of) Visions. Our first tagline was "Question what is--imagine what if..."

The connections between art, society, and social change intrigued Russell, and he thought hard about how people might use art as a vehicle for change as well as how to get artwork out of the rarefied art world through cross-disciplinary initiatives. Shortly after its first five years of operation, PL became an independent entity. Russell moved the library to the Art & Design building at George Mason University (GMU) in Fairfax, Virginia, a diverse community with a large immigrant population (about 50% of GMU students are people of color), where it now houses a collection of over 7000 items related to art and social change. In addition to the collection, it offers programs, events and presentations that explore the connection of art and change. It also holds exhibitions of socially engaged art. Through the years, the original mission for PL remains intact, but it has grown to encompass a diverse palette of initiatives and collaborations with students, artists, and community members, both locally and globally.

The library currently consists of a tight 400 square foot space packed with the collection and a long table. It is open access and used for study, research, and meetings. Student interns assist Russell with PL's day-to-day operations. According to Russell, the organizing principle behind the library is a set of social change themes called the Meridians: "The rubric that we have [has] 33 subject areas called Meridians that guide our collections policy. It is really [used] to serve [and] guide all of our policies. If we are going to do a project, it is always in relation to some combination of the 33 Meridians." These themes are not comprehensive, but correlate to "pressing social issues while encouraging cross-fertilization and holistic approaches to social change projects across sectors and disciplines" (Provisions Library, 2012b). Examples of Meridians include "Free Expression," "Oppression," "Radical Education," and "Rights of Humans."

Introductory art classes at GMU's School of Art introduce students to ideas they might not easily find on the Internet, and PL is a space where they can further their research and think about the content and context of their academic and creative work. Russell finds that many art schools are oriented towards teaching styles and techniques, but that PL adds another layer, engaging students with their art through the lens of society and culture. He encourages students to think about art beyond the gallery wall. The student-run Mason Mural Brigade (http://www.gmu.edu/org/muralbrigade/), for example, brings student and professional artists together in social exploration through creating murals on campus and in their community. Russell collaborates with these students and artists, helping them with their designs, providing them with feedback, engaging their critical thinking skills, and expanding their consciousness.

Russell also works with departments outside of the School of Art, collaborating with students from Geographic Information Systems, Mathematics, Chemistry, Engineering, and Social Psychology. The projects are usually in the medium of sculpture and focus on solid and visual representations in the form of shapes, plate tectonics, or biological structures. Eventually Russell would like to get university funding to support even more multi-disciplinary engagement across departments.

PL extends its reach beyond the campus. In 2007, it worked with a GMU faculty member on the Floating Lab Collective (FLC) (https://floatinglabcollective.com/), a program devoted to direct action within the community through the mediums of social research and artwork. FLC projects have exhibited in Washington D.C. as well as South America. To date, the collective has developed over 50 groundbreaking community projects. Russell described a project they did in Medellin, Columbia,

> We did our largest project in Medellin, Colombia in 2012. It was called The Collective White House. We engaged with six different neighborhoods. Six projects were brought together in the main square of the city in a one sixth-scale replica of the White House made out of bed sheets. It is like the idea of creating an imaginary government with imaginary agencies that are in different neighborhoods. Those agencies would generate projects and then they would be gathered together in the main government buildings. We were always looking for opportunities like that, but that was a super exceptional one. [The project] was about empowering communities. Not so much about coming in and bringing things, but going in and listening. Finding people with an idea and empowering them to realize it.

There are opportunities for collaboration beyond GMU, as evidenced by Russell's conversations with many visitors who have said how they would like to have a PL in their own communities. Russell noted, however, that although the library coordinates exhibits all over campus, it is not terribly well known to the wider Fairfax community, and that location is currently a challenge to gaining wider audience. Although the performing arts are quite popular in Fairfax, fine art has not had the same amount of success. This challenge, however, is an opportunity, as one of the reasons Russell located PL in a suburban area was to expose the community to the art scene and cultivate their interest. Projects like the aforementioned Mason Mural Brigade should help in that regard, bringing more visibility to art in the community. After 18 years of cultivating a viable resource and art center, Russell plans to keep reaching out and he is enthusiastically open to new collaborations.

Russell wants to one-day expand PL beyond its current cramped quarters in order to further such community collaborations. There are, for instance, local art organizations that the library has not yet worked with, but would like to in the future. To facilitate such partnerships,

Russell envisions relocating the collection to a multi-purpose "art science society museum" with ample space to display collaborative research and art projects.

Donald Russell has lived in Washington D.C. since 1980 where he was formerly the Director of Washington Project for the Arts. He also worked with the National Endowment for the Arts and the Smithsonian Institute before co-founding Provisions Library with Gaylord Neely in 2001. In addition to directing the library, Russell is University Curator for George Mason University.

2.11.1 Takeaways

- Transformative library and information projects must extend past walls to offer support, education, and inspiration to the wider community. They should not allow institutional boundaries to limit whom they reach.
- Collaboration with artists, campuses, and communities can destroy silos and incubate knowledge.
- Art and activism complement one another. Art creates social interaction that leads to awareness and change, and information organizations should facilitate this reciprocal action.

2.12 Slab City Library: with Cornelius Vango, Librarian (Aug. 28, 2018)

https://www.facebook.com/Slabcitylibrary/; https://squattheplanet.com/atlas/slab-city-library.2/

Slab City, often referred to as "the Slabs" by residents, is a decades old squatter community located in California's Sonoran desert about 150 miles East of San Diego and 50 miles south of Joshua Tree National Park. It sits on the footprint of Camp Dunlap, a decommissioned US Marine Corps base, and got its name from the concrete foundations left over from the base that are now used as spots for permanent and seasonal residents to set up their camps. Dubbed "the last free place in America," the Slabs is an uncontrolled community. The lack of official government means no rent or landlords, no parking lot fees for recreational vehicles and trailers, and the opportunity for people to find freedom and refuge away from the restrictions and contradictions of modern society. This freedom also means that there is no electricity, sewage, or other utilities beyond what people provide for themselves. The desert heat is brutal during the summer months, reaching up to 130 °F, but the milder winters make the location attractive to snowbirds (people who move to warmer southern climates during the winter months). During the winters, the population swells to as many as 2000 people, but there are between 100 and 150 year-round determined residents (slabbers) that have chosen to live in the Slabs out of economic necessity or the desire to live an alternative, off-the-grid lifestyle.

Many people go to the Slabs to escape from traditional society, some go there to embrace anarchist living, and some just go there to be left alone. It is a community with its own businesses, music venues, and restaurants. There are fantastic art installations like East Jesus, a sprawling communal project composed of salvaged objects, and the towering Salvation Mountain, a three-story, rainbow-colored clay monument. One successful project is Slab City Library, which provides residents with access to a rich collection of reading material as well as acts as a community center for residents, a recreational spot, a movie theater, a music venue, a bar, and a resource for free materials like clothes, shoes, food, and other items. What Slab City Library does not have, nor does it miss, is the effluvium associated with capitalist institutions.

Cornelius Vango, a painter, multi-media artist, nomad, and Internet presence as a videographer and entertainer, had been going to the Slabs for three winter seasons and learned about the library in 2013. Rosalie, a Slab City resident and librarian by trade, had built the library in 1999. However, when Rosalie passed away in 2003, it went largely abandoned until enjoying a brief resurrection in 2013 when two men had begun trying to restore it. Looking to get off the road for a while, Vango decided to stay in the Slabs for a time to work on some projects and possibly start an art gallery. Friends suggested, however, that since Vango loved the library, why not bring it back to life? Having inspected it during the season, Vango decided to move in when they limped their dying van to it in the fall of 2014. Vango said that

> When I pulled my broke down van into what is kind of its driveway, I got a flat tire, like hardcore flat. My van said "Okay, this is where I am going to be," and I kind of took it as a big omen. I was like "I guess I am about to post up here for a little while." I did not have any money to fix the van, and it would take a long time to figure out how to get out of that situation.

Committing to rebuild the library, Vango regularly hitchhiked to the nearby towns Niland, Brawley, and El Centro in order to get supplies. They also used their YouTube channel (https://www.youtube.com/channel/UCh3SpI_QxJvaPb9S2IiU0JQ) to bring awareness to the project. Soon other people, both slabbers and folks living outside of the Slabs, began to get excited about the project. Shortly after Vango took over operations, for instance, the library received a literal truckload of science, philosophy, and political books from the estate of a college professor who had recently passed away. Through such donations, the ready availability of volunteer help, and Vango's own dedication and hard work, the library now provides patrons with free access to a collection of nearly 5000 books.

At Slab City Library there are no due dates or library cards. In fact, with the exception of a small, non-circulating ready reference collection, people are not expected to return the books that they take out. This policy makes sense when considering the nomadic lifestyle of many of the folks that come through the library, many of whom would hesitate to borrow something that they may have limited opportunities in the future to return. The lack of restrictions on library services also mirrors the slabbers' *de facto* anarchist ethos, their desire for freedom, and disdain for a bureaucracy that its residents seek to escape and make unnecessary. Vango explained this practical approach to anarchism and how the library fits into such a scheme:

> I am the one running [the library]. I can make it my own because it is the space that I occupy. That is what autonomy is. It is self-governance in the space that you occupy. I have allowed other people into my space to occupy it alongside of me, but I do not lord my position over them. They are members of the household as well. So it is more like a tribe or a family where we get together and we talk, and people are perfectly welcome to say "hey Cornelius, you need to shut up, you are stupid, and you are wrong," and I will say "oh well, why don't you tell me what you think. What's your alternative to that?" We will talk it out like family members in a functioning collective.

The library, therefore, is a collective of anarchist punks like Vango at the same time that it is Vango's year round house. It sits at the center of an area in the Slabs known as Libraria, a "micro-nation" stretching over an approximately 2.5 acre patch of land. Within Libraria there are different camps that people occupy on a temporary basis (when they leave a camp, Vango decides who uses it next). Residents make their own decisions within the spaces that they occupy, and this system operates upon mutual respect, not codified regulations. "When I go to somebody else's house," Vango said, "even though it is still in my yard, it is Libraria. That is their house. I cannot go and start telling people to do dishes at their camps. That is just not how it works."

A major obstacle that Vango faces running the library relates to the slabbers' alternative approach to living and the preconceived notions of many people coming from outside of the community, many of which have been negatively influenced by how the media portrays Slab City. Vango has encountered rude people with skewed ideas of how to behave in the Slabs:

> *You have to give people some rough lessons sometimes because they think that no law enforcement equals lawlessness. [. . .] But when you are in another person's space in an anarchist situation, that other person has just as much freedom to act and react as you do. So, if anything, there is more law because everybody enforces their own personal law in the space that they occupy. I find myself explaining that a lot to people.*

Through Vango's efforts and community buy-in, Slab City Library continues to be successful. At this point, Vango has to tell people not to bring in more truckloads of books because the library does not have the space to house more of them. Now they are trying to distribute the books as quickly as the items come in. Slab City Library is also in cooperation with the website Squat the Planet (http://squattheplanet.com), a "community of do-it-yourself nomads" (Squat the Planet, n.d.), and many of Squat the Planet's members come out to the library to help out as volunteers. For the past four years, the library has also been hosting the Squat the Planet Jamboree, which Vango said is a lot of work but an exciting experience and a privilege to be involved with. Vango also continues to update their popular YouTube channel, which provides insight into the library, Slab City, and the nomadic lifestyle.

Slab City Library thrives, and it does so in a way that sits in stark contrast to the public libraries with which most people are familiar. Vango refused to conform to the limits and hierarchies imposed by modern capitalist society, and has realized something that has beaten the odds. While the library is a prefigurative institution in an anarchist sense, modeling how society *should be*, it is also an organic part of the community within which, and for whom, it arose. It supplements the information needs of people with limited access to traditional library services, and it does so without imposing upon them any of the coercion associated with government backed ideological institutions.

Cornelius Vango is an artist living in Slab City, California. Vango re-established the Slab City Library in the fall of 2014 and currently lives and works there as its librarian.

2.12.1 Takeaways

- Government or corporate funding is not necessary for the success of a library or other information service. Do-it-yourself!
- Libraries themselves can transcend the role of state and government institutions.
- Examples of functioning, practical anarchism exist and demonstrate how libraries can be organic to the communities that they serve.

2.13 Southern California Library for Social Studies and Research: with Yusef Omowale, Library Director (Sept. 24, 2018)

6120 S. Vermont Avenue, Los Angeles, CA 90044; (323)-759-6063; http://www.socallib.org/; archives@socallib.org

Located in South Central Los Angeles, an area known for economic disinvestment, violence, police oppression, and now gentrification, the Southern California Library for Social Studies and Research (SCL) was established by Emil Freed in 1963 as a community based non-profit organization. A Communist Party member, community organizer, and social justice activist, Freed amassed archival materials relating to social struggles from all over the world, collecting pamphlets and other political material in an effort to preserve the historical legacies of leftist movements. By1970, the collection warranted a permanent space, and Freed purchased the location in South Central where the library resides today (Southern California Library, n.d.).

The SCL collection is rich with materials that relate to civil rights events, the Unemployed Councils of the 1930s, and the Civil Rights Council of the late 1940s and early 1950s (Cooper, 1990). Freed also preserved thousands of penny pamphlets from "labor organizing campaigns, civil rights cases, and the significance of Marxism to present-day America," amassing an impressive collection of U.S. labor history related materials (Danky, Cooper, & Embardo, 1989). Pamphlets in the collection represent labor organizations such as Industrial Workers of the

World, United Auto Workers, International Ladies' Garment Workers Union, and the United Steel Workers of America, to name a few (Cooper, 1990). In addition, SCL curates local collections, including the Hollywood Studio Strikes collection, which contains material chronicling Freed's own arrest outside of Columbia Studios, and the legal papers of Attorney General of California Robert W. Kenny, which preserves documentation of activists' efforts to fight against immigrant deportation (Danky et al., 1989). The library also has a robust collection of films, photographs, and community programing materials.

SCL's collections reflect the people in the surrounding neighborhoods and are grounded in the history of their lived conditions. SCL Director Yusef Omowale told us that the library staff—currently just himself and Communications Director Michele Welsing—maintains a close relationship with the local community, which in turn helps them develop and optimize their holdings. Omowale stressed the necessity of building collections that are of significance and value to the community served: "For us, that is more important than just being a repository or preserving materials. We really want to find ways to engage [the public] and have the materials inform and inspire people who are working to create change, now." One ongoing effort of SCL, for example, is to help organizations fight gentrification issues in Los Angeles. Not only are communities facing upheaval, arrests have increased as part of what some see as an effort by developers to remove "unacceptable" residents. Community members, especially those with criminal histories, have been targeted in raids and seek out SCL as a safe haven and a place to organize. With more funding, Omowale would like to develop these collections into robust information resources that local residents can use when facing gentrification concerns.

Although SCL is enmeshed within the community it serves, Omowale said that it is "not tailored to the community," i.e., the library often seeks to challenge the traditional narratives held by many of its members concerning their "innocence." He contends that other advocacy groups will sometimes make a generalized claim of innocence and legitimacy in their community, which can actually be harmful to residents. Such narratives may inform many of the residents of South Central Los Angeles, but all residents may not be "innocent" in the traditional sense. Many have committed crimes or have been to prison, and a problematic narrative of "innocence" reduces one's ability to advocate for all segments of the community. Omowale prefers to work side by side with locals to clarify narratives and understand needs.

The library is a daily stop for many residents in the area, especially those facing the harshest impacts of late capitalism, and it also functions as a resource center for the public by offering services to those experiencing homelessness, hunger, and other forms of trauma. For instance, SCL organizes food and clothing drives, with community members taking donations to the people who need them or inviting them to visit the library to collect the items. In addition to local residents and community organizers, researchers seek out the collection from across the United States as well as from other countries. The library attracts many activists, authors, academics, educators, filmmakers, and artists, a diverse range of people who take advantage of both its holdings and meeting spaces.

There are no professional archivists on staff and volunteers do most of the collection processing. Omowale sometimes collaborates with local colleges' service learning programs and community volunteers to organize things. For example, the 100 + box Coalition Against Police Abuse collection, one of SCL's most used collections, was processed by young people taking part in a summer youth employment program. Such community engagement, he said, is ideal because, "we would like the community that we work with to also be involved in the production of the archive, not just using it."

Community engagement is also vital to the library because the challenges that SCL face are aggravated by the small size of its staff. Omowale, for instance, does not actively take part in a significant amount of outreach due to time demands. Nevertheless, even without constant outreach, SCL averages a healthy influx of visitors. This is because local patrons and community members help by spreading the word, in effect doing most of the outreach as volunteers. For example, Omowale told us about a local college faculty member and their graduate students who were collecting oral histories for a project. A community member canvased the area and recruited many members of the community to offer their stories.

Again, largely because of the small staff size, many of the library's holdings remain unprocessed, with more urgent community needs many times taking precedence over collection processing. This backlog often makes discovery through traditional methods a time consuming process. Although academic researchers are typically more familiar with the organization of research collections, a community organizer or K–12 teacher may need additional assistance in finding items, and it may take the staff a few days to locate materials for an event or classroom exercise.

Furthermore, since the library is independent and unaffiliated with any institutions in the area, communication gaps sometimes arise, placing additional stress on SCL staff. College instructors, for instance, often assign their students projects requiring them to visit the library and find articles for their topic, and Omowale and Welsing do not always receive direct communication to anticipate their needs.

Finally, because, colleges and universities are more frequently earmarking funds to obtain collections pertaining to the labor struggles and social injustices of marginalized communities, and because obtaining funding for SLC collections can be difficult, important collections can get bought up and effectively locked away:

> There is a lot more interest, particularly from large funders, to diversify archives, and more attention paid to so-called community archives and marginalized history. [. . .] Communities and organizations like ours have been supporting and sustaining these histories for decades and generations. Now you have universities getting $450,000, $250,000—money like that—to begin acquiring community archives. The money is not going to organizations like ours or other communities that have been sustaining these histories [. . .]. Essentially, we look at it like [the universities are] colonizing the community archive. It is an urgent time to figure out what to do about that, because you cannot really compete with an institution that has thousands of dollars to get archives.

Omowale fears that universities, which can afford to purchase collections from people who are looking to monetize their collections, will buy up the bulk of the material, and that the level of restrictions found at many university archives will prevent access and usage. Because of this trend, SCL's long-term goals center on sustainability. Even though the library has been operating for over 55 years, Omowale said that it remains in survival mode: "I think for us, those larger goals are trying to figure out how to move from survival to intentionality. Where we are able to do more of proactive outreach; we are able to go out and begin building and developing the archives that we want." Omowale said that the organizations like SCL, unlike many large universities, have the advantage of being able to develop community relationships that are extensive and deep, and that the residents, local activists, and visiting researchers are what keep the library an important fixture of the surrounding neighborhoods.

Yusef Omowale is only the third Director of the Southern California Library in the past 56 years, and, although he does not have a formal background in library science or archival certification, his commitment and knowledge of the organization is essential to forwarding SCL's mission. Omowale has many influences and cites Nina Simone, James Baldwin, Audre Lorde, Fred Moten, Saidiya Hartman, Katherine McKittrick, and Clyde Woods. Omowale also credits the residents in South Central Los Angeles as greatly influencing the trajectory of his life. They heavily influence his work as well as the mission of SCL.

2.13.1 Takeaways

- Community archives are an integral part of local residential areas, providing resources to the residents that clarify community narratives. One should not hesitate to use a community archive as a means to challenge that community.
- Community archives are not *just* archives. They should comfort community members in need through services that address quality of life issues.
- Community volunteers can help promote a project, connect residents with services, and serve as ambassadors to attract engagement with the local information literacy programming.

References

ABC No Rio. (n.d.). About. Retrieved from http://www.abcnorio.org/about/about. html.

Abram, D. (1997). *The spell of the sensuous: Perception and language in a more-than-human world*. New York, NY: Pantheon Books.

Andersen, L. (2003). Expanding our work with prisoners. *Progressive Librarian, 22,* 62−64.

Andersen, L. (2012). Moving on -- Or how I left a truly great job for extraordinary insecurity. *Progressive Librarian, 38/39,* 64−68.

Bales, S. (2018). *Social justice and library work: A guide to theory and practice*. Oxford, UK: Chandos Publishers.

Balsamini, L. (2012). Libraries and archives of the anarchist movement in Italy. *Progressive Librarian, 40,* 1−15.

Barnard College. (2018). About the college. Retrieved from https://barnard.edu/about/about-the-college

Barnard Zines Library. (2018). About zines at Barnard. Retrieved from https://zines.barnard.edu/about-zines-at-barnard.

Bartel, J. (2004). *From A to zine: Building a winning zine collection in your library*. Chicago: American Library Association.

Buchanan, R. J. (2018). *Writing a riot: Riot grrrl zines and feminist rhetorics*. New York: Peter Lang.

Cooper, S. (1990). Sources on labor history at the Southern California Library for social studies and research. *Labor History, 31*(1-2), 208−212.

Cornell University Library. (2018). Finding textbooks in the library: Cornell Lending Library. Retrieved from https://guides.library.cornell.edu/textbooks.

Danky, J. P., Cooper, S., & Embardo, E. E. (1989). Resources for scholars: Collections of alternative and left materials, Part 1. *Library Quarterly, 59*(1), 47–63.

Durland Alternatives Library. (2018). Home. Retrieved from https://www.alternativeslibrary.org/.

East Side Freedom Library. (n.d.-a). About us. Retrieved from https://eastsidefreedomlibrary.org/about/.

East Side Freedom Library. (n.d.-b). East side freedom library: 5th Anniversary Celebration featuring Jelani Cobb. Retrieved from https://www.youtube.com/watch?v = 2yWdiAYrUY4&t = 3s.

East Side Freedom Library. (n.d.-c). ESFL collections. Retrieved from https://eastsidefreedomlibrary.org/collections/.

Erickson, C. (2018). *Environmental justice as social work*. New York, NY: Oxford University Press.

Freedman, J. (2006). A DIY collection. *Library Quarterly, 131*(11), 36–38.

Freedman, J. (2009). Grrrl zines in the library. *Signs: Journal of Women in Culture & Society, 35*(1), 52–59.

Freire, P. (2018). *Pedagogy of the oppressed* (M. Bergman Ramos, Trans.). New York, NY: Bloomsbury Academic.

Gaut, G. (2019). *Reinventing the people's library*. St. Paul, MN: East Side Freedom Library.

Gordon, B., Hanna, L., Hoyer, J., & Ordaz, V. (2016). Archives, education, and access: Learning at interference archive. *Radical Teacher, 105*, 54–60.

Groeneveld, E. (2016). *Making feminist media: Third-wave magazines on the cusp of the digital age*. Waterloo, ON: Wilfrid Laurier University Press.

Hays, A. (2017). Reading the margins: Embedded narratives in feminist personal zines. *Journal of Popular Culture, 50*(1), 86–108.

Hmong Archives. (n.d.). About. Retrieved from http://hmongarchives.org/about/.

Interference Archive. (n.d.-a). Our Mission. Retrieved from http://interferencearchive.org/our-mission/.

Interference Archive. (n.d.-b). Volunteer. Retrieved from http://interferencearchive.org/volunteer/.

Ishizuka, K., & Stephens, R. (2019). The cat is out of the Bag: Orientalism, antiBlackness, and white supremacy in Dr. Seuss's children's books. *Research on Diversity in Youth Literature, 1*(2), 1–50. Retrieved from https://sophia.stkate.edu/rdyl/vol1/iss2/4/.

Jaeger, P. T., Taylor, N. G., & Gorham, U. (2015). *Libraries, human rights, and social justice: Enabling access and promoting inclusion*. Lanham, MD: Rowman & Littlefield.

Klein, N. (2007). *Shock Doctrine: The rise of disaster capitalism*. Toronto: A.A: Knopf Canada.

Moran, J. (2016). To spread the revolution: Anarchist archives and libraries. Retrieved from https://theanarchistlibrary.org/category/author/jessica-moran.

Petrossiants, A. (2017). Resistance across time: Interference Archive. *Brooklyn Rail*. Retrieved from https://brooklynrail.org/2017/11/artseen/Resistance-Across-Time-Interference-Archive.

Provisions Library. (2012a). About. Retrieved from https://provisionslibrary.org/about/info/.

Provisions Library. (2012b). Meridians. Retrieved from https://provisionslibrary.org/about/meridians/.

Southern California Library. (n.d.) About us. Retrieved from http://www.socallib.org/scl-about.

Spunk Collective. (2002). Spunk Library. Retrieved from www.spunk.org.

Squat the Planet. (n.d.). Welcome to Squat the Planet. Retrieved from https://squatthe-planet.com/.

St. Lifer, E., & Rogers, M. (1994). Finger Lakes alternative. *Library Journal, 119*(2), 25.

Wertham, F. (1973). *The world of fanzines: A special form of communication.* Carbondale: Southern Illinois University Press.

Further reading

Radway, J. (2016). Girl zine networks, underground itineraries, and riot grrrl history: Making sense of the struggle for new social forms in the 1990s and beyond. *Journal of American Studies, 50*(1), 1−31.

CHAPTER THREE

Advocate: transformative library and information projects reaching out

3.1 Introduction

The profiles in this chapter cover 13 library and information science related projects that provide resources and services to their constituencies in novel ways to support justice related change:

1. ATD Fourth World Street Libraries
2. Awesome Foundation, Awesome Libraries Chapter
3. Ferguson Municipal Public Library
4. Freedom to Read Foundation
5. Laundromat Library League
6. Liberation Library
7. Librarians for Social Justice
8. Libraries Without Borders
9. Library Freedom Project
10. National Coalition Against Censorship
11. Progressionista
12. Street Books
13. Whole Person Librarianship

Many of these projects serve particular at-risk populations such as the poor and economically disadvantaged, those currently experiencing homelessness, children and young adults, the incarcerated, and refugees and immigrants. Libraries Without Borders (LWB), for example, sets up its IDEAS boxes—self-contained mobile media centers and libraries—in areas inhabited by victims of natural disaster and war such as Haiti following the 2010 earthquake and Syrian refugee camps in Iran. While LWB is an international organization operating many national affiliates, we also include spunky little startups like Detroit, Michigan's Progressionista, which introduces pre-teen girls of color to both literature and professional women of color, and Portland Oregon's Street

Transformative Library and Information Work.
DOI: https://doi.org/10.1016/B978-0-08-103011-0.00003-4
© 2020 Elsevier Ltd.
All rights reserved.

Books, which sends out bike-pulled libraries to serve that city's large population of those currently experiencing homelessness.

Other groups that we profiled do not advocate for any one specific at-risk population. For instance, although the New York City-based National Coalition Against Censorship prioritizes schoolchildren in K-12 educational settings as part of its mission to defend free speech rights, that is by no means its only constituency. Alison Macrina's Library Freedom Project, inspired by the Eric Snowden affair and working to protect individual privacy rights, aims explicitly at the larger library using public. Awesome Foundation Libraries supports many different constituencies through its micro-grant awards that incubate projects embodying diversity and inclusivity.

All of the organizations in this chapter are essentially grassroots projects and initiatives. Some are well established, having been around for decades, while others have been operating for only a few years. One common thread that runs through all of these organizations, however, is that they all began as the passion project of one or just a small number of people that saw a lacuna in today's society in need of attention. Sarah Zettervall's Whole Person Librarianship, for instance, was inspired partly by her experiences doing a library school internship at juvenile detention facilities. There she collaborated with social workers, demonstrating to her the need to explore potential partnerships between library work and social work. Awesome Foundation Libraries came out of the work of three library workers who wanted to help prototype innovative ideas and encourage risk taking with minimal repercussions on the part of the innovators. Possibly one of the most inspiring organizations that we profiled is the Ferguson Municipal Public Library (FMPL), which, through the efforts of its staff, local schoolteachers, and volunteers, showed how a community could come together in the face of crisis and pain to begin the process of healing itself. Scott Bonner, FMPL Director, told us that the experience was "kind of glorious." The same might be said for every other project profiled here.

3.2 ATD Fourth World Street Libraries: with Karen Stornelli, USA National Director of ATD Fourth World (July 18, 2018)

PO Box 1787, Gallup, NM 87305; (505)-488-3624; https://www.atd-fourthworld.org/; nationalcenter@4thworldmovement.org

Founded in 1957 by Catholic priest Joseph Wresinski in an emergency housing camp near Paris, France, ATD Fourth World (the ATD stands for "All Together in Dignity") is an international organization dedicated to the eradication of extreme poverty through the promotion of culture and education, people-centered and earth-friendly development, and the advancement of human rights and peace (ATD Fourth World, n.d.). The organization currently has Volunteer Corps teams in 32 countries spread across five continents, the Indian Ocean, and the Caribbean. Teams take part in multiple different projects, campaigns, and advocacy efforts designed and implemented in partnership with people experiencing poverty. One long-running effort (since the 1960s), and a signature program of ATD Fourth World, are their Street Libraries. These libraries provide poor and low-income children and their families with access to books, art, and fun educational activities. The libraries are set up in their users' neighborhoods, in partnership with community residents, to bring services directly to the point of need.

Karen Stornelli is currently one of the National Directors of ATD Fourth World USA and Director of local programs in New Mexico. Drawn to social justice work while in college, she did an internship with ATD Fourth World in 1996. Attracted to the international scope of the organization, its dedication to community engagement, and the opportunity it provides for long-term options for engagement, she spent the next 22 years working for rural and urban communities in the United States, West Africa, and Europe. Stornelli said that the Street Libraries reflect ATD Fourth World's belief that people require more in their lives than just basic needs; they should have access to culture and connections to learning and knowledge. Realistically, the provision of such access means bringing services directly to the community members themselves, many of whom might not have the means to travel far for resources. In New York City, for instance, the ATD Fourth World Street Library sets up at the center of the Brownsville housing project, a low-income community. In Gallup, New Mexico, where Stornelli works, the Street Library is located in a vendor stall at the local Gallup Flea Market. The key to selecting a location, she said, is visibility:

> We generally pick a very visible place, a place that is outside and a place that is accessible to families that will not be able to go very far. If you imagine communities disproportionately affected by violence and crime, you are not wanting kids or families to have to go too far. In any case, they won't [travel too far]. They have their comfort zone based on their knowledge of their community,

so we pick locations where people can feel that they have an eye on what is going on. Doing that also helps to lead to parental and community involvement. It generally starts with children coming out to the library. Little by little, as families watch and observe, they get involved.

At the Gallup Flea Market, the Street Library, officially named the Story Garden, provides a shady area with bookshelves, games, and activities. There is an art table, a puppet theater, collaborative games, a touch screen computer, and sandboxes for the little children. A donated trailer provides a quiet space for reading inside. ATD Fourth World has worked over the years to make the Street Libraries intergenerational spaces, and library space is structured to accommodate from the youngest babies to great grandparents. This was done, Stornelli said, because they realized that people were coming to the library as extended families. Families visiting the flea market may stop by Story Garden for a few minutes or up to several hours at a time. Children of vendors also frequent the space. Families may travel from three to four hours away to sell at the flea market, bringing their children with them, so Story Garden is something for the kids to do while their parents are selling at the market.

Successfully meshing with the community that they serve is an important part of these Street Libraries' success, and successful collaboration with the community requires deep community involvement and commitment. Although the Gallup Story Garden takes place only on Saturdays, preparation goes on throughout the week. Not only must materials and tools be prepared for the weekend, it is necessary to engage continuously with the community, and ATD Fourth World makes every effort to involve parents and community members along the way. The Volunteer Corps members may, for instance, visit a parent and ask them to help run an activity the following week, or to see if they are going to encourage their child to come out and take part in activities. An important element of ATD Fourth World's trust process with the community is giving roles, even leadership roles, to parents or other community members (the NYC and New Orleans Street Libraries, for instance, tend to attract many students as volunteers) who are interested in becoming further involved. Stornelli said that,

We generally set up Street Libraries so that we are in a position where we really need the community, and we do. I mean that when we are out in these communities, we need the community on board and to be supporting—either with issues that might come up, or with, for example, giving us electricity from their apartment or water or whatever. So, there are smaller and then bigger ways that people will show their support for what we do. It does revolve around the community, community involvement, and showing the community that they have knowledge and skills and value that they can share with others.

Fostering community involvement can be challenging. Stornelli said that often the adult community members—the parents, the grandparents, and others—feel that they do not have much to contribute; they may not have had the chance to feel like they were valued citizens with something to give back:

I think that is a large obstacle in terms of community involvement, just really convincing people that they have something to bring in regardless of their educational level. People sometimes feel intimidated when they do not know how to read and write or they did not complete their schooling, and they feel as if they have nothing to teach children. So that process of trying to convince them that we are not the experts, that we need them, and they have something important to share with the youth in their communities is challenging.

Successful collaboration also requires recognition by those coming from outside a community that, to make a service successful, they must also learn from the people that they serve. ATD Fourth World USA intentionally incorporates reflexivity into its operating procedures in order to maximize benefits to those people served, as well as consolidate and build upon what they themselves have learned. This learning happens with community, parents, and other volunteers who are part of the facilitation team. This praxis involves the facilitators composing weekly interaction reports in which they summarize what they have experienced and learned. They then share their experiences during a weekly team debriefing session. Stornelli said that during these debriefing sessions,

We each share some points from what we have written and we reflect on what that means for going forward, what we learned from this, and how we can improve our practice. It is a reflective practice cycle that we try to really incorporate week by week. And then a couple of times a year through a slower kind of planning process we will go back and look more at these reports we have written and think about direction or change. If you can imagine it, maybe a grandparent mentioned some kind of idea that they think would be interesting and you hear it in one ear but you are busy. So later you write it out and you think "oh wait, so-and-so suggested this, let's put some thought into it." We will think about it, and the following Saturday we may go back to the grandparent and say, "tell us more about your idea." It is a way for us to build on what we are learning.

This highly coordinated and regular reflective process helps the ATD Fourth World Team fully integrate what they are hearing from people and what they are learning. Stornelli said that it also helps the team track their progress over time: "We might notice with a child who cannot read that a year later they are eager to read and they are doing a good job."

When asked what advice she has for those individuals or organizations contemplating projects similar to the ATD Fourth World Street Libraries, Stornelli stressed the necessity to develop the community's trust. An important aspect of building and maintaining this trust is maximum visibility, which is a key requirement for any organization when a project is trying to reach people who are not being reached by the services, resources, and structures that already exist. Story Garden has had to resist the invitations of well-intentioned people to move them into an inside location protected from the weather, but less visible and accessible to families. While Stornelli said that this is a lovely idea, it will not work because it is the mission of ATD Fourth World to reach people who are not being effectively reached for a variety of reasons by the services, resources, and structures that already exist. By going into the community, the organization becomes more thoroughly integrated with that community and is ultimately more effective. Building trust, she said, also requires that one adopt a nonjudgmental approach and that "when we go in looking for what is wrong with a community, then this approach of building trust and collaborating with the community is just not going to work." Stornelli recommended that activists demonstrate to the people they are working with that they are there to learn from community members, are willing to follow their lead, and respect and need community members' opinions. Finally, Stornelli said that consistency and the establishment of long-term commitments to projects are necessary for gaining trust. Low-income areas often see programs and projects come and go. To be successful, she said, one has to be ready to stick it out with the community. The fact that ATD Fourth World's Street Library programs have been operating for decades is a testament to the effectivity of their philosophy and methods.

Karen Stornelli is a Volunteer Corps member with ATD Fourth World, a human rights and social justice organization working to overcome extreme poverty (4thworldmovement.org). Since 1996, Karen has been part of ATD's Street Library program in the US, Europe, and West Africa, bringing educational and creative-expression resources into the heart of under-served communities, from open-air rural markets that are hubs for the social and economic life of the community, to low-income, isolated urban neighborhoods. Karen is passionate about engaging with community members to design and implement knowledge-sharing programs that respond to their aspirations and draw out their unique knowledge and skills.

3.2.1 Takeaways

- Libraries and information services owe more to people than just their basic needs.
- Providing effective services means setting up where the people you serve feel most comfortable, not where you feel most comfortable.
- Engaging in structured reflective practices will help your organization or project evolve and adapt to the needs of the community it serves.
- Build community trust through visibility, remaining nonjudgmental, and being committed and consistent.

3.3 Awesome Foundation, Awesome Libraries Chapter: with Robin Champieux, Joshua Finnell, and Bonnie Tijerina (Chapter Deans) (June 21, 2018)

https://www.awesomefoundation.org/en/chapters/libraries; https://www.awesomelibraries.org/; libraries@awesomefoundation.org

The Awesome Foundation (https://www.awesomefoundation.org/en) is an international organization that awards no strings attached microgrants of $1000 to help fund projects that advance "the interest of awesome in the universe, $1000 at a time" (Awesome Foundation, n.d.-a). It is made up of individual, autonomous chapters, each of which is composed of 10 "trustees" in charge of raising the funds for the individual grants, reviewing project proposals, and awarding the money to successful applicants. It is the Awesome Libraries Chapter's (ALC) mission to "provide a catalyst for prototyping both technical and non-technical library innovations to embody the principles of diversity, inclusivity, creativity, and risk-taking" (Awesome Foundation, n.d.-b).

All Awesome Foundation chapters are founded and managed by "Deans." We spoke with ALC's three Deans, Robin Champieux, Joshua Finnell, and Bonnie Tijerina, about the chapter's origins, objectives, funded projects, and challenges faced. The idea to start ALC germinated in the work that Champieux, Finnell, and Tijerina were doing in the non-profit organization Library Pipeline (https://www.librarypipeline.org/), an organization that supports innovation in library work by bringing together disparate groups to consider ideas in the library field that needed to be examined or even solved. Prior to becoming an official Awesome Foundation chapter, ALC began as a Library Pipeline pilot program based on the Awesome Foundation model. Finnell explained that:

> We all came together under the Library Pipeline Innovation Group. As we were thinking through ideas, the idea for a micro-funding campaign really started to gain traction amongst the members [. . .]. Within this group, we started to put together our initial trustee list and started to winnow down this large amorphous idea of creating a small funding space for creative projects to something that could actually blossom on its own.

Champieux said that the idea for starting up a micro-funding project was appealing because such initiatives could help prototype innovative ideas and support risk taking with minimal repercussions in the event of failure. There would be no huge application to complete, and the funding amounts are so modest that if an initiative does not get off the ground or it fails, the experience and the investment in the innovation is still a win. The three approached The Awesome Foundation in 2016, and the organization was open to having a library-themed chapter. The Deans then recruited trustees, figured out what types of grants they wanted to fund, collected the money, and moved forward. Tijerina said that working with an established organization like The Awesome Foundation brought with it certain advantages. The organization already possessed an existing infrastructure. It also had a well-established online presence and was capable of pushing out open calls for micro-grant proposals.

ALC, however, is somewhat different from the other Awesome Foundation chapters. First, it is one of only four (out of 96) "worldwide" chapters, the other 92 being regional, usually city-based chapters. Because diversity and inclusivity are principles that its trustees want embodied in the submitted projects, the Deans thought that the trustees themselves should also represent diversity and inclusivity. Therefore, Finnell said that when the Deans put out an initial call of trustees, they were intentional in identifying people worldwide that would make good trustees.

> In addition to soliciting trustees around the globe, and from different libraries and life experiences [. . .] we also discussed the meaning of these principles that we have set for ourselves: diversity, inclusivity, creativity, risk-taking. Instead of providing prescriptive definitions of these terms, our hope was to recruit a diverse trustee group to come together and talk about those principles through the grant applications we were evaluating together.

In addition to its status as a worldwide chapter, ALC has more than the 10 members that make up the typical Awesome Foundation chapter. This increased number of trustees lowers the barrier for entry and means that individuals are not required to contribute as much money per month to make up the grants. This is an important modification when one considers that library workers, which comprise most of the chapter's trustees, tend to be serially underpaid. Furthermore, following the six-month long pilot project, Tijerina said that ALC decided to award its grants quarterly instead of monthly: "We realized it was a ton of work to do every month. Part of it is because we are virtual. If you look at the Awesome Foundation, most of their chapters are in a city, so they gather once a month, have a meal or a drink, and then vote." ALC members, however, live around the world, which requires additional logistical considerations. Another unique feature of the chapter is that it allows people and groups to sponsor seats during the quarterly votes held to award grants. Sponsored seats are a way for people from around the world who may not otherwise have the necessary funds to have a say in the process. Finally, Tijerina said that the Deans have recently held a live pitch event at the American Library Association Annual Midwinter Conference in order to involve and animate the larger community of library and information workers:

> We want to get the traditional library community inspired by other people's ideas and to think, "Oh, I do have a little project but I have not really put that out there." We worked through the [American Library Association] Center for the Future of Libraries. Miguel Figueroa, who is the Director of the Center, is one of our trustees. He is a big supporter of what we are doing and helped organize the pitch event. We had ten project pitches, and then we had the library community who was in the room vote for their favorite. It was a way to get the profession, even those who would not normally think about getting a small project or idea funded, excited about their colleagues' projects and excited about projects they might have. It was a lot of fun.

ALC has currently funded eight Awesome Library projects, many of which relate to social justice issues. Supported projects have included The Library for Food Sovereignty, which is building a digital library of information concerning grassroots farming technologies, Progressionista, an organization that is also profiled in this book (see page 106), and the Greece-based Melissa Network Reading Corner to Deconstruct Gender Roles. While the ALC Deans find it difficult to pinpoint any one project as a favorite, Champieux said that it is particularly exciting when she sees communities and people that are not library workers thinking about how a library could help a community's needs:

> In some ways, those are the most inspiring projects for me because it is a group of people saying, "Oh, one thing that will help us heal and make this community thrive is a library." These are libraries as they conceived them or sort of a library-like service as they imagine it. That just blows my mind, and it is so cool.

Being an ALC Dean is a lot of work and includes sending out the collected grant proposals to chapter trustees, making sure that ALC's social media presence remains updated, and fundraising for the sponsored seats. Managing the quarterly grant-making process is also time-consuming. The three Deans must get together, winnow down the large number of grant proposals to 30 or so reasonable applications, send out the voting poll to the trustees, and then organize all of the trustees to meet at a reasonable time to discuss and vote on an awardee. Given the international character of the ALC trustee cohort, this last effort involves working across multiple time zones. According to Finnell, "things kind of hum along for three months. We get in grant proposals. We read them. Some of them we decide to discard, others we think will be great, and those are the pool for our discussion. But a lot of our time is kind of flat and then ramps up and then kind of flattens again."

Funding is an ongoing concern. Finnell sees funding not as an obstacle, but as a challenge to surmount. Having to be selective about awards has resulted in a productive dialogue among trustees about the project's core principles; it is "a good constant challenge that we are always thinking about, thinking through, and trying to improve." Champieux underscored the value of an open communication model that keeps organizational core values and mission front and center. Having mission-focused conversations when opportunities or challenges arise keeps things from spinning off in too many different directions. Tijerina noted that such steady collaboration with like-minded comrades is ultimately one of the most rewarding aspects of the project.

> I have done other things where I built something from scratch. I have done them alone and with other people. The advice that I would give somebody is to try hard to find your people, people that think as you do, because there is a lot of work involved in building something that does not yet exist. Finding like-minded people will reduce the amount of work and make the process more fun, interesting, and inspiring. It matters a great deal.

ALC demonstrates that big ideas and big results are not solely the domain of big organizations with big money. Small teams of dedicated people, strengthened by diversity and inclusiveness, can achieve awesome results.

Robin Champieux is the Research and Open Science Librarian at Oregon Health & Science University.

Joshua Finnell is the head of research and instruction and an associate professor at the university libraries at Colgate University in New York. He co-founded the Awesome Libraries chapter of the Awesome Foundation in 2017. His work has appeared in *SCRIPTed: A Journal of Law, Technology & Society, New Library World, Public Library Quarterly, and Reference Librarianship & Justice: History, Practice & Praxis.* He was named an Emerging Leader by the American Library Association in 2009 and a Library Journal Mover and Shaker in 2012. He is currently the associate editor of *Global Knowledge, Memory and Communication.*

Bonnie Tijerina is a librarian, entrepreneur, and library community convener. She is currently a researcher at the Data & Society Research Institute in New York City. She is founder of ER&L (Electronic Resources & Libraries) conference and organization, created to facilitate communication and foster collaboration among information management and e-resources professionals in libraries. Bonnie has worked in academic libraries for over ten years and is Principal Consultant and Founder of the Library Consulting Network and a Trustee of Awesome Libraries.

3.3.1 Takeaways

- Consider collaborating with existing organizations in order to benefit from their experience, expertise, and infrastructure.
- Think global. Diversity and inclusivity, while logistically challenging, will ultimately be more fruitful.
- Design your project to fit your project team. Propose operating structures outside of the norm if they appear to be a better fit for the situation.
- Remember to keep your core mission and principles a part of your group's ongoing decision-making processes.
- Seek out and find "your people" as colleagues and project collaborators. It results in less work and more fun.

3.4 Ferguson Municipal Public Library: with Scott Bonner, Director (June 1, 2018)

35 North Florissant Road Ferguson, Missouri 63135; (314)-521-4820; http://ferguson.lib.mo.us/; Twitter@fergusonlibrary

On August 9, 2014, the United States took pause when Darren Wilson, a white police officer, fatally shot Michael Brown, an 18-year-old African American in Ferguson Missouri. Questioning the use of deadly force, the local community rallied around Brown's family and, on the Sunday morning following the shooting, protests broke out in Ferguson with citizens chanting, "We want answers" and "No justice, no peace" (Salter, 2014; August 10). Ferguson Municipal Public Library (FMPL), guided by Director Scott Bonner, leapt into action to support the city's struggling citizens.

Ferguson is an independent municipality located in St. Louis County, and FMPL is an independent library working with a consortium of other independent public libraries in the county. Bonner said that,

> Being an independent library means that we can focus all of our attention on the people of Ferguson and really care about our community deeply. [We] have the freedom to try new things, make things up, and go our own path without having to answer to a big bureaucracy or having to worry about how we are divvying up resources among various locations.

Bonner reports to a nine-person board of volunteers that approves of his passion for civic engagement. He said that in 2014 he had just been hired as Library Director and "I was brand new to everyone... people didn't know me yet, and so I kind of was able to take risks, lots of risks, and be allowed to take risks." For example, Ferguson is a city with a majority African American population, but one that is represented politically by a predominantly white leadership structure. Since this disparity can be challenging for the citizens of Ferguson, Bonner created programming both on how to run for office and on voter registration resources. The Michael Brown shooting, however, prompted a new level of engagement on the library's part that further empowered the Ferguson community to call for justice and change.

When the shooting happened, FMPL had a small staff and limited resources. Bonner said that the media took the few incidents of fires, looting, and rioting that occurred during the protests and sensationalized them. The majority of the protesters, he said, were peaceful, and daily life in Ferguson was less dangerous than how it was reported in the news. Every day following the incident, Bonner assessed the local landscape and safety of his staff and patrons, his mantra becoming, "If safe, open. If open, do everything we possibly can." He wanted the public library to be many things for the community: a place to rest and recharge, a center for support and community unification, and a resource to help meet the needs of citizens during a period of public strife.

For months after the shooting, FMPL created and collaborated on hundreds of community programs. The most pressing need at the time, Bonner said, was supporting the educational requirements of local school-children. The Ferguson–Florissant School District was scheduled to begin its school year on Thursday, August 14, 2014, but, due to the shooting, it announced closure for that week and, surprisingly, the next. Despite the upheaval, Bonner used social media, Twitter and Facebook, to get the word out that the library would remain open. Bonner said,

> All these kids have no place to go. Which means all these parents are left in a lurch. If you are working three part time jobs to make ends meet, and any one of these jobs can fire you for any reason or none, being unable to show up for all your jobs because you have not secured childcare yet really matters.

As Bonner strategized just how to meet the needs of the families of Ferguson, Carrie Pace, an Art Teacher at Walnut Grove Elementary School, approached him with a possible solution to the problem. The two developed an ad-hoc school, with Pace providing local teachers who wanted to tutor students during the closure and FMPL providing both the space and resources for them to do so. The project became the School of Peace, even making the national news (CNN Wire, 2014). Although only a few dozen kids showed up on the first day of operation, the volunteer teachers were adamant about getting the word out, holding signs out by the street advertising the make-shift school as both a space for free learning and a safe place for parents to leave their kids while they went to work. Every day the number of schoolchildren grew, and soon more teachers from the school district, retired educators, and volunteers from the nonprofit organization Teach for America (https://www.teach-foramerica.org/) showed up to help. In the morning, parents dropped their kids off in the care of teachers who guided them in math, science, and literature activities. Teenagers even volunteered to help with the younger children. Bonner and the volunteers met every morning to coordinate food, snacks, room assignments, and activities for the day, and then met again at the end of the day to plan for the next day. All of this, Bonner said, "was kind-of glorious."

As the School of Peace started taking off, the media focused their attention on its sign-wielding teachers. One day, as Bonner brought water to the teachers outside, a camera operator approached him saying, "It has been a week. We need a change in the story. You are it." Following that interview, reporters and cameras soon packed the library, and Bonner had to act as gatekeeper to the press due to patron privacy concerns. The press coverage, as well as the library and volunteer efforts, triggered donations of "books, supplies, and lunches for the kids. . . from individuals and organizations such as Teach for America, the Saint Louis Science Center, Operation Food Search, and the Missouri National Park Service" (Inklebarger, 2014, p. 17). By Wednesday of the second week of school closure, the School for Peace was at near capacity, and the next day, it expanded into the First Baptist Church down the street. In this effort, approximately 100 teachers kept over 200 students in school while providing their parents with a way to stay working.

Bonner said that even though staff and volunteers often worked 16-hour days, rarely saw their families, and routinely went home exhausted, it was all worth it. Not only did the community hold FMPL in high regard, but donations also started to pour in from across the country. Bonner credited staying open throughout the first days of the trauma even remaining open the night of the grand jury announcement, with transforming FMPL into a radically different sort of library: "Whenever other people were closing up, boarding up, and trying to trying to hide-...we left our windows uncovered, opened our doors wide, and [said] 'we're here for you.'" The donations allowed FMPL to hire full-time staff, and Bonner was able to convert some part-time staff into full-time positions, reinforcing day-to-day consistency and professionalism. These adjustments also gave FMPL employees some breathing room and the mental space to concentrate more on improving the library, as opposed to just trying to make it through a shift.

The donations also allowed the library to update the physical structures and resources within the library. Bonner was able to replace damaged carpet and 20-year-old HVAC units as well as update exterior doors to provide accessibility for disabled patrons. With grant monies and a donation from Hewlett-Packard, FMPL replaced public service and staff computers and obtained a smart board, narrowing the digital divide for patrons.

Now, with its boosted level of service and community-focused librarianship, Bonner knew that FMPL must actively work to maintain this "new normal." In 2018, the library worked with the organization EveryLibrary on a campaign to put a tax levy up for vote that would allow FMPL to maintain this better-funded existence (Sweeney, 2018). The measure passed with 66% of the votes, and Bonner felt that the library had proved itself to the community:

> When you get out to know the community and get to know people and figure out their needs and then try to make a program that meet their needs… This very community-focused kind of librarianship changed the nature of how we interact with the community that we live in, the kind of space our community can have, and what the library could do for them.

Collaborating with the community is an essential component of FMPL's success. After the influx of donations, Bonner was also able to hire a full time Children's and Programming Librarian. This library worker does most of her outreach away from the building, reaching children by going directly to Ferguson's public schools, private schools, and daycare centers. FMPL also collaborated with church day camp programs; setting up scavenger hunts and visits to the library, worked with Ferguson Youth Initiative (https://fyifergyouth.org) to place book boxes around the city for immediate access to reading materials, and hosted the US Small Business Administration for two weeks, providing a space for citizens to apply for emergency loans. It also assisted with a multi-location art show, working with the Alliance of Black Art Galleries and providing the library building as the flagship location for the event. Reflecting on FMPL's response to the Michael Brown shooting and aftermath, Bonner said,

> There was always this message of inclusiveness and acceptance, which is politically charged. It is definitely politically charged to say we welcome everyone and that everyone is welcome here. But, it is the kind of politically charged statement that we get away with because we are a library. Libraries are supposed to be inclusive. […] so part of what was making all of that tricky is to stay politically neutral while doing all of these things that are not neutral.

As FMPL finds more support within the community, Bonner and his staff will continue to work hard to meet the community's needs. In 2015, *Library Journal* named FMPL Library of the Year (Miller, 2015).

After working with adolescents in the mental health field, Scott Bonner obtained his master's degree in information science from the

University of Missouri–Columbia and went into library work. He worked at St. Louis Public Library System and as the Adult Services Librarian at Richmond Heights Library in St. Louis County before becoming Director of Ferguson, Missouri's Ferguson Municipal Public Library in 2014, where he continues in this position.

3.4.1 Takeaways

- Regardless of whether you succeed or fail, take risks. Doing so can create opportunities.
- Collaborating with outside organizations can help a project design services to support their patrons, and tailoring programming to a community creates value and buy-in for the citizens who use a library's services.
- Going beyond the physical library and encountering patrons in their own space brings education and resources to their door.
- Even when things are difficult, assess the situation and, if it benefits your community, do whatever you can to "Get Open."

3.5 Freedom to Read Foundation: With Deborah Caldwell-Stone, Executive Director, and James Larue, Former Executive Director (Sept. 30, 2018)

50 East Huron St. Chicago, IL 60611; (312)-280-4226; (800)-545-2433 ext. 4226; https://www.ftrf.org/; ftrf@ala.org

Founded in 1969, Freedom to Read Foundation (FTRF) sprang out of library and information workers' dedication to freedom of information, and its slogan, "free people read freely" reflects the organization's efforts to fight for the First Amendment rights of readers. FTFR supports libraries' right to collect materials without hindrance and the rights of individuals to access those materials without restrictions, as well as freedom of speech and freedom of the press. The organization was born when members of the American Library Association (ALA) became increasingly concerned about having the "adequate means to support and defend librarians whose positions are jeopardized because of their resistance to abridgments of the First Amendment; and to set legal precedent for the freedom to read on behalf of all the people" (Freedom to Read Foundation, 2019a). Although FTRF is affiliated with ALA's Office for Intellectual Freedom

(OIF), it is a separate 501c3 non-profit organization and maintains its own membership and services to constituents. Deborah Caldwell-Stone, FTRF Executive Director, explained that through their services,

> FTRF wants to guarantee that all individuals have the right to express their ideas without government interference, and to read and listen to the ideas of others. The Freedom to Read Foundation was established to promote and defend this right and to foster librarians and libraries as institutions where every individual's First Amendment freedoms are fulfilled. Their mission is to support the right of libraries to include and make available any work in their collections that they may legally acquire.

FTRF membership has fluctuated over the years, being anywhere from 800 to 1500 members and, although it consists mostly of library workers, there are also lawyers and journalists who join the organization. Members defend First Amendment initiatives directly and through monetary support.

FTRF focuses on three main areas of intervention: (1) aiding in litigation that directly supports and affects freedom of speech, (2) making grants and scholarships to individuals and groups in support of projects affiliated with free speech initiatives as well as of travel to professional conferences, and (3) educating about the First Amendment's relationship to libraries and information access.

FTRF aids in litigation that directly supports and/or affects freedom of speech. The cases that FTRF pursue can be controversial, addressing issues such as controversial speech, animal cruelty, and revenge pornography. Unlike ALA, whose support is typically narrower in scope and focuses primarily on libraries and library workers, FTRF frequently teams up with groups like the Media Coalition and Comic Book Legal Defense Fund to preserve First Amendment rights. They also support journalists in litigation when there is a threat to their ability to perform their jobs.

The organization has been involved in several notable cases. In *Doe v. Gonzales (2005)*, for example, they aided the Connecticut Four, a group of library workers challenging the constitutionality of certain provisions in the USA PATRIOT Act. Caldwell-Stone detailed how FTRF worked with American Civil Liberties Union attorneys to help the defendants:

> FTRF provided support to attorneys representing the Connecticut Four, [Doe v. Gonzalez], the four librarians who challenged a national security letter order that was issued to the Library Connection Consortium in 2005 requiring them to turn over records under the PATRIOT Act. We provided amicus support through briefing and resource support to American Civil Liberties Union

attorneys representing those librarians. So, the Foundation has served as a legal support for libraries, librarians and the First Amendment generally over the decades. We do have a timeline that identifies the cases that FTRF have been involved with over the decades and you will find a mix there of both library cases and more general First Amendment cases that the Foundation has litigated.

The Connecticut Four successfully litigated against a USA PATRIOT Act–authorized national security letter (NSL), with the court finding that the gag order associated with the NSL violated the First Amendment rights of its recipients (Kelley, 2013, June 18). Former FTFR Executive Director James LaRue told us:

I really do believe that this is in many respects the key contribution [of] The Freedom to Read Foundation, the willingness to go to court to defend these things. We have noticed that publishers or other people out in the for-profit world, they like having the Freedom to Read Foundation there because it carries with it that wonderful image of librarians. So, we bring the public good whenever we attach our name to one of these free speech issues. I really do think that is our claim to fame.

Laws can be so broadly written that they restrict First Amendment freedoms, and, in turn, prevent libraries from providing materials to patrons. In 2014, Arizona passed House Bill 2515, a statute that would have criminalized the distribution of any image of a nude person without the subject's consent. The bill's language was so broad that library workers who loaned or provided access to images, such as the famous nude image of a young girl fleeing a napalm strike in the Vietnam War, could be prosecuted in criminal court. FTRF became a plaintiff in that lawsuit, Antigone Books v. Brnovich (2015), in order to defend both the library worker's right to distribute that material and the library user's right to access it. In 2015, the law was permanently halted (Media Coalition, 2019).

The Foundation's greatest legal success came in 1997 with *Reno v. American Civil Liberties Union* (1997). FTRF and the ALA were leading plaintiffs in the case, which challenged the 1996 Communications Decency Act (CDA). Theresa Chmara (2017, June 26), FTRF's general counsel, wrote, "The CDA made it a crime to place content on the Internet that was 'indecent' or 'patently offensive' if that content would be accessed by minors under the age of 18." FTRF argued that the statute violated the First Amendment and filed a lawsuit on behalf of libraries, library users, and FTRF members. On June 26, 1997, the United States Supreme Court held that the First Amendment applied without limitation to the Internet and that the CDA violated the First Amendment (Chmara, 2017).

In an ideal world, FTRF would have cooperating attorneys in every US state to assist library workers and library trustees with censorship challenges. Right now, with a small three-person office, the best that Caldwell-Stone and her two colleagues can do is offer legal resources and make the best referrals they can. They are not, however, without allies. The organization, for instance, works closely with the ACLU. One case they assisted the ACLU with was *PFLAG v. Camdenton R-III School District* (2012), in which a high school used Internet filters to block students from accessing materials that presented pro-LGBTQIA + (lesbian, gay, bisexual, transgender, pansexual, genderqueer, queer, intersex, agender, asexual, and ally) views of civil rights issues such as same sex marriage. The case was resolved by a judgment in favor of the students, and Camdenton R-III School District had to stop using the discriminatory content filter (American Civil Liberties Union, 2019b). While FTRF supported the ACLU's case through amicus curiae briefs, Caldwell-Stone noted, "We really wish we could have been there on the frontlines representing the library ourselves rather than working through a proxy."

Achieving less media attention, but also of great importance, is FTRF's support of First Amendment rights through their awarding grants and scholarships. The Judith Krug Fund, established to advance former FRTR Director Judith Krug's commitment to educating librarians about intellectual freedom and First Amendment issues, underwrites grants to support libraries and schools sponsoring ALA Banned Books Week events. Applicants may apply for grants of up to $6000 for promotional activities that focus on the censorship of books that have been historically, or are currently, banned from schools, libraries, and other public repositories. The FTRF's awards its annual Gordon M. Conable Conference Scholarship to provide travel to library school students or new librarians to the profession to attend the ALA Annual Conference. The scholarship goes to a recipient who is interested in mentoring and education towards intellectual freedom.

Lastly, FTRF actively works to educate people about intellectual freedom and privacy, collaborating with the University of Illinois Urbana-Champaign and San José State University to offer online courses to future information professionals. The intent of the program is to prepare students to understand issues surrounding First Amendment rights, privacy, intellectual freedom, and censorship in the context of access to information (Freedom to Read Foundation, 2019b).

FTRF are hoping that, through recent donations and cultivation of future donors, they can increase the level of support that they provide in censorship cases, particularly by engaging with school boards and school districts to defend minors whose rights have been violated. They also hope to put together a series of webinars designed to educate library workers and other information professionals about First Amendment rights. Both Caldwell-Stone and Larue envision that the organization will create more educational materials—possibly a book series—to provide library workers with a more complete and definitive source of information to understand things like copyright, liability, and the current legal environment. As a longer-term goal, they anticipate developing similar programs and materials for lawyers to help them learn more about First Amendment issues related to libraries, with the hope that these legal professionals will in turn provide pro bono support to information institutions facing challenges such as censorship.

Deborah Caldwell-Stone is the Executive Director of the Freedom to Read Foundation and the Director of the American Libraries Association Office of Intellectual Freedom. Caldwell-Stone holds a JD from Chicago-Kent College of Law at Illinois Institute of Technology and was formerly an attorney in a private practice. She has been with the FTRF and ALA since 2000 where she advises on law and policy regarding free expression and privacy issues. She also works with the FTRF's eleven-member board of trustees on litigation and policy matters.

James LaRue is former Executive Director of the Freedom to Read Foundation and former Director of the American Libraries Association Office of Intellectual Freedom. In 1981, LaRue recieved his Master of Library Science from the University of Illinois, Champagne-Urbana, and he has worked as an academic librarian and reference librarian before serving as the Director of the Douglas County Colorado Libraries for 24 years. Larue's book, *New inquisition: Understanding and managing intellectual freedom challenges* (Libraries Unlimited, 2007) describes his experiences fighting for intellectual freedom and advocating for First Amendment rights. In 2018, he departed from ALA and FTRF to work as a writer, speaker, and consultant.

3.5.1 Takeaways

- Fighting for individual freedom of expression is a necessity.
- If you witness or experience infringements on First Amendment rights, speak up and, if possible, bring your project's resources to bear on the situation.

- Consider teaming up with non-library related groups that share similar goals and objectives.

3.6 Laundromat Library League: With Arlene Rengert, Co-Founder (May 22, 2018)

http://laundromatlibraryleague.org/; laundromatlibrary@gmail.com

Started in 2014 by Arlene Rengert and Karen Iacobucci in West Chester, Pennsylvania, the Laundromat Library League (LLL) is a grassroots organization dedicated to promoting literacy among children who may not have ready access to books at home. The beginnings of the idea came when Rengert attended a social gathering and chatted with a woman who was placing free children's books in community-based locations. She thought this was a clever notion, and that laundromats would be an ideal place for children to have access to reading materials while their parents did the wash. Although West Chester is a wealthy suburb, there are still areas in the community where residents rely heavily on laundromats. People who use laundromats on a regular basis, she said, "usually do not have home laundering appliances and are less likely to have children's books there, or the leisure time to take children to libraries." Rengert tucked the idea away, but eventually floated it to her close friend Iacobucci, who also saw value in placing books in laundromats. Rengert and Iacobucci brainstormed ideas and subsequently convinced a local washateria owner to allow them to put a decorated cardboard box full of children's books inside his establishment. A local elementary school librarian was enthusiastic about the project and provided them with their first donation: three boxes of books from Chester County's Downingtown Elementary School. LLL has not stopped growing since.

The program has expanded remarkably in size by word of mouth, with people learning about LLL and volunteering to develop book boxes for their local laundromats. For example, one man from New Jersey discovered an LLL box at a West Chester laundromat and contacted Rengert about setting up a box back home to serve low-income residents. Such volunteers, or "stewards," replenish the box or boxes twice a month. Rengert was recently astonished to learn that former running back for the Philadelphia Eagles, James Betterson, highlighted the LLL box in one of his laundromat's promotional YouTube videos. Many stewards take on a laundromat close to their home or on their way to work, and even if there is not a robust community of participating laundromats nearby, LLL can be a self-starter initiative. One volunteer, a librarian in Navajo County, Arizona, started a LLL book box approximately 60 miles from the nearest library, providing much-needed children's books to several isolated reservations. As of summer 2019, LLL has developed a diverse network of over 450 volunteers (many of whom Rengert has never met) that maintain boxes at 181 laundromat sites in 21 states across the United States. LLL also works to make its stewards' financial burden as light as possible:

> [We] will pay postage and will direct mail books, "book stickers" [identifying items as part of the program], and laminated signs for the boxes so that the volunteer's financial burden is only the cardboard box. However, in most cases volunteers offer to print stickers and signs at their location. [LLL provides templates for this purpose through their website]. LLL also offers resources and guidance to volunteers that wish to become self-sufficient in obtaining books from sources in their own communities.

The organization maintains a selection process for the books they put in the boxes, and every box placed in a laundromat starts out with a curated collection of 60 books for children aged toddlers through teens. The titles cannot have a religious theme; this prevents a laundromat from declining based on their own belief system. On their monthly visits, stewards remove any adult books, whether they are notable titles or not, that have made their way into the boxes. Children need not return books to the boxes, and Rengert said, "For the past two years, every book that we put in the boxes has what is called a book sticker on the front of it. [The stickers] are actually labels that have our website and logo. . . and it simply says: 'read it, love it, pass it on.'" When a box is depleted to two-thirds its original size, it is replenished with a fresh inventory of 60 items, and any leftover books are remixed into other collections.

So far, LLL has received over 84,000 books through donations. Nonetheless, Rengert said that they get very few items in Spanish, and that few donated books, in fact, present much in the way of "ethnic diversity or heroes of color or heroines of color." They also need more toddler board books, and Rengert constantly keeps an eye out for bargains, buying up specials on books that fit into the age categories and sought after themes. LLL, as a result, welcomes books or financial donations that will help them obtain more titles with diverse characters and topics.

Rengert and Iacobucci incorporated LLL into a 501c3 non-profit organization, with a twelve-member board that meets once a year to advise the organization. The program receives roughly $3200 per year in donations to cover their annual operating budget, and all proceeds go towards purchasing books and maintaining the organization's Web presence. Several organizations contribute to the program, and LLL has received donations from the local Chapter of the American Association of University Women, the Chester County Reading Association, a university retired faculty group, local chapters of Business and Professional Women's Club, Delta Kappa Gamma (an international woman educators association), several faith communities, and individual donors. Assistance is not limited to monetary donations alone. For example, the program has an agreement with Better World Books (https://www.betterworldbooks. com/) where they can have all the free "gently used" children's books they need as long as LLL pays for postage, and this partnership helps get books to participating locations in distant states. LLL encourages donations to support the organization's efforts through newsletters, emails, and social media, and Rengert drums up support with presentations to churches, volunteer groups, and country clubs. To help further with costs, the program holds restaurant fundraisers about 10 times a year to bring in monetary donations as well as events like a recent Giving Tuesday Facebook appeal that collected over $1000.

Although Rengert has experienced plenty of generosity while running LLL, there are the occasional laundromat owners that prefer not to have the boxes in their establishment, as well as a few instances where volunteers have reported that their boxes have disappeared. Nonetheless, the overall success rate has been remarkable and the program is thriving. LLL recently received a grant in 2019 from the Lang Family Foundation to underwrite costs for 20 new locations in states not contiguous to Pennsylvania. The funding will help support the purchase of books, labels, and other supplies. As LLL expands, Rengert continues to connect willing volunteers to a meaningful organization that gets books into the hands of children. She said that her ultimate goal is to have "at least one laundromat in all 50 states some time before I die. My more immediate goal is that I would like to have 200 sites, and I think we are going to get there. This is my gut feeling...that this seems to be taking off."

Growing up in Illinois, Arlene Rengert was an avid reader from an early age, riding her bike to the town library and reading almost every book in the stacks. Rengert earned her doctorate from the University of

Pennsylvania and was a professor of Geography at West Chester University, from which she has since retired. She has always cared about children and social justice and, after leaving Illinois for East Pennsylvania in the 1970s, felt newly empowered and began volunteer work and taking part in organized protests. Rengert is married and has five children.

3.6.1 Takeaways

- One can start community-based organization with very little resources.
- A healthy network of volunteers can be nurtured through online resources and support, and a project can cultivate effective volunteers without necessarily ever meeting them in person.
- Volunteers will participate when they are given the agency to develop their own initiative under a wider organizational umbrella.

3.7 Liberation Library: with Stavroula Harissis, Former Steering Committee Member (July 16, 2018)

2040 N Milwaukee Ave, Chicago, IL 60647; http://www.liberationlib.com/; liberationlibraryil@gmail.com

The United States has the dubious distinction of maintaining the highest rate of imprisonment in world. It also has the highest number of incarcerated youth in the world, with "nearly 53,000 youth [being] held in facilities away from home as a result of juvenile or criminal justice involvement" (Prison Policy Institute, 2018). According to the American Civil Liberties Union (ACLU), in 2013, the state of Illinois had a youth incarceration rate of 169 per 100,000 people, with 1617 persons in juvenile facilities and 68 persons in adult prisons (American Civil Liberties Union, 2019b). The state's incarcerated youth, nonetheless, have dedicated advocates. The Chicago based Liberation Library was started in 2015 by Project NIA, a youth advocacy group that works "to meet the needs of victims, reduce recidivism, and improve satisfaction with the legal system" (Project NIA, n.d.). Liberation Library is an all-volunteer organization that provides youth incarcerated in all Illinois prisons and juvenile detention facilities with access to reading material. At first, none of the original volunteers were professional library workers (there are now several library workers involved with the program). They were and remain, however, prison abolitionists advocates of social and restorative justice, providing books while at the same time working to get rid of prisons altogether.

Stavroula Harissis was on the Liberation Library steering committee from 2017 to 2018 and continues to volunteer for the organization on various projects. As a Marxist and long-time social activist, Harissis sees the program as supporting her belief that people must work together to realize a more just and fair society. As a library worker—a program librarian at a public library—she was drawn to the Liberation Library, seeing the project as a valuable intersection of social justice and library work. There are many library programs in the US that provide prisoners with access to books, but Liberation Library is somewhat different than most. This is because instead of just sending extra books to prisons and detention centers, the imprisoned Illinois youths actually request the books of their choice directly from the organization. The incarcerated young people fill out a form providing Liberation Library with a list of their top three reading choices as well as general information about what they like to read so that volunteers can work with them to match their needs. The books (all of which are donated to Liberation Library) are then packaged and sent out to the prisons twice a month. This operational model allows the kids to receive books that they want to read, providing them with some agency in the process. Harissis said that

> Many of the youth facilities [in Illinois] do have libraries and some sort of educational system setup within them. They are not completely without access to information, but it is very limited and sort of restrained. So, I think that the gap that we fill is that it is really about respecting [the incarcerated youths'] agency. You have been in a cage. You are told what to do and what not to do, and no one really respects your opinion. [...] It is more than just books. When you listen to and respect their opinions, they will be more likely to connect with you in the future and take your suggestions.

Young, Phillips, and Nasir (2010) found in a qualitative case study of a youth prison that prison schooling bolsters institutional control while reinforcing the stigmatization of students as convicted criminals, and that "institutional goals often trumped the educational goals and played a strong role in the prison experience for students" (p. 219). It has been argued that personal agency and autonomous decision making, as opposed to the strict structural control typically associated with the modern prison system, develops a juvenile's ability to exercise "prudential risk choice," that is, their capacity to make good personal decisions (Kemshall, 2008, p. 23).

Every package that Liberation Library sends out is both desired by and individualized to its recipient. Books even include a handwritten note from a Liberation Library volunteer because, Harissis reiterated, "it is more than just sending books to them. It is a way to create a connection to the outside world for them." The letters, she said, are not the "sorry that you are in jail" type, but instead "are more about the books themselves and making a connection with [the youth], like if the volunteer writing the note has read the book before, they might write what they liked about it or a similar comment to really engage them as readers." The benefit that the Liberation Library provides young people through its distribution practices (by giving the books to youth to keep) cannot be overstated. The incarcerated young people are both included in the process and treated as individual human beings.

Liberation Library is coordinated by a steering committee of eight members and supported by numerous volunteers. There is neither a hierarchy to the steering committee, nor officers. They meet once a month in person, but the bulk of the work happens through a project-based approach that capitalizes on the particular skills of committee members. For example, one person may focus on social media while another person focuses on building connections with outside organizations. A large concentration of the work happens on twice monthly "packing days" where steering committee members and other volunteers (around 10 non-steering committee volunteers sign up for every packing day, and these are usually different people each time) get together to go through requests, get books from Liberation Library's stacks, pack them up, and send them out. Outside of packing day, Liberation Library does a lot of social media work maintaining their website as well as different projects and campaigns, many times in collaboration with outside partners.

Working with incarcerated youths can be a daunting task. Liberation Library has a contact within the Illinois Department of Juvenile Justice that has been a key element to their success. Working within the individual facilities, nonetheless, can be challenging. Each facility is somewhat different, and they sometimes come up against resistance. Such resistance usually comes down to push back against the kind of books that the program is sending over, leading to rejections of some books that the patrons request. Considering that Liberation Library is staunchly against censorship and upholds the freedom to read, it has become part of their struggle to fight against prison censorship of the books that they are sending out. Sometimes conflicts can be resolved through dialogue. The organization has engaged in successful conversations with facilities to justify reading materials deemed controversial. One advantage, therefore, of having added several professional library workers to the steering committee is that such representation strengthens the organization's ability to persuade others concerning the value of controversial reading material. Harissis noted that the committee is

> also working on updating our catalog with books that we can say that... this [catalog] was developed by librarians who have a knowledge of [children and young adult literature] and preempt the censorship issue in that way by providing book options recommended by librarians. We try to get the conversation moving that way.

Despite the occasional hitch caused by institutional censorship (something familiar to people in most lines of library work), Liberation Library has been enormously successful at what they do, receiving substantial support from the public and attracting many volunteers. For example, a recent project where they solicited help for a holiday card writing campaign resulted in a flood of donated holiday cards—many more cards, in fact, than there are incarcerated youth in Illinois. They ended up, as a result, sending many of the donated cards to partners in other states. The twice-monthly packing days are also a popular draw for volunteers, with participation slots filling up quickly. Harissis, however, does not see the organization expanding geographically, but as instead concentrating on making a deeper impact within Illinois. A lot of what the steering committee is doing now, she said, is thinking about ways to expand the program and extend its mission and impact by thinking "bigger about ways to grow and what other campaigns we can develop to inspire this growth. We have been talking about doing a One Book, One Community program. Trying to get permission to go into facilities to be able to lead a full discussion with the youth. We haven't gotten that going yet, but that's kind of the vision."

Over the past few decades, the concept of restorative justice has seen an upswing in interest among political conservatives and liberals alike (Braithwaite, 2002), and access to information should be a key part of any project aimed at healing both individuals and communities. Imprisoned youth are easily lost in the judicial system and risk becoming institutionalized at a pivotal moment in their development. Library and information workers have a responsibility to advocate for marginalized and at-risk populations. The American Library Association states in *Access to Library Resources and Services to Minors: An Interpretation of the Library Bill or Rights,* "Librarians and library governing bodies have a public and professional obligation to ensure that all members of the community they serve have free, equal, and equitable access to the entire range of library resources regardless of content, approach, or format" (American Library Association, 2014). The *Interpretation* also advocates for the non-censorship of materials to prisoners regardless of age (American Library Association, 2019). Library and information workers should look to Liberation Library as an example of how to serve the information needs of this serially underserved population.

Stavroula Harissis is a former steering committee member of Liberation Library, a volunteer-run organization in Chicago that provides books to young people in Illinois prisons and juvenile detention centers (http://www.liberationlib.com/). She currently works as a programming librarian at Indian Trails Public Library in Wheeling, Illinois and serves on the Action Council of the Social Responsibilities Round Table of the American Library Association. As an activist, she has worked on numerous campaigns in support of the labor movement and social justice causes, particularly in the areas of education, economic justice, and anti-fascism.

3.7.1 Takeaways

- Recognize the importance of patron agency and autonomy, work towards it, and be prepared to fight for it within systems that encourage structure and conformity.
- Treating patrons as individuals helps to benefit them through personalization of service.
- A project's lack of internal hierarchy, as well as eschewal of such an administrative structure, may serve as an excellent foil to the structure of neoliberal institutions like prisons.
- Increasing a project's impact does not necessarily correlate with an increase in its geographical reach.

3.8 Librarians for Social Justice: with Kelly Grogg, Founder and Former Chair (Nov. 9, 2018) and Rebekah Walker, Founding Member and Former Chair (Nov. 8, 2018)

https://www.slis.uiowa.edu/current-students/lsj; libs.social.justice@gmail.com; https://www.facebook.com/groups/765131470351319/?ref = br_rs; zine@abcnorio.org

Based at the University of Iowa School of Library & Information Science (SLIS), Librarians for Social Justice (LSJ) is a progressive organization that "focuses on the many social justice issues librarians face in the workplace" (Librarians for Social Justice, n.d.). For this profile, we interviewed Kelly Grogg, founder and former Chair of LSJ, and Rebeka Walker, a founding member and the (now former) Chair that followed immediately after Grogg in 2016.

While studying at the SLIS in 2015, Grogg, a former Peace Corps volunteer and presently digital librarian for the US Public Broadcasting Service, had a guest speaker visit her SLIS Community Engagement class and discuss their work with a local men's prison book club. Intrigued, she talked more with the speaker after class and then started helping out with the program. In addition, she completed an independent study related to community engagement. Because of these experiences, Grogg began developing the idea for the action-oriented, student-based (but not limited to students, library workers are also welcome to join) organization with the goal of creating community-based change. The group's catch phrase is "more information, more action."

Grogg said that Iowa City, Iowa is noteworthy because of the large number of library workers employed in its public libraries, the university, and the State Historical Society, professionals particularly suited to be involved with social justice initiatives because of their passion for public service. The SLIS also meant the presence of a number of library school students, many of whom were looking for practical work experience, and this suggested the possibility of collaboration and learning between the two groups:

> We have all of these librarians in Iowa City, and we also have all of these library school students, and I think one of the biggest frustrations for library school students was their lack of hands on, concrete experience in libraries. Unless you were lucky enough to get one of the few student worker positions at the time, you were not getting many hands on experiences that were going to be necessary for you once you graduated and started looking for a job. I knew that there was a community need [for SLJ], and I knew there was also this need for library students to be more involved [with the community]. I thought it would be interesting to try to work with librarians and library students [in ways] where we could do different community projects loosely related to librarianship. That way people can get experience, and we can be of some service to the community.

Grogg put out a general call to SLIS graduate students, an organizing meeting followed, and LSJ began its work in 2015. Operating a largely student-based group has both advantages and disadvantages. A major positive is that library school students tend to be passionate, to bring excitement to projects, and they are hungry to gain experience. Grogg noted that although she was concerned that no one would show up for the first LSJ meeting, people did. Importantly, people continued to show up consistently after that initial meeting. Both Grogg and Walker, however, remarked on the fact that student populations are transient groups, with graduate students usually staying for two or three years and then moving on to begin their careers. Grogg said that the generally rapid turnover of SLIS cohorts was among her biggest concerns:

> It was my second year [in the master's program], and I did not want to have this group for a year and people be like "it is Kelly's group so when she leaves it is not going to happen anymore." So, I made it really clear from the beginning that I started this, and it was my idea, but I am not the leader or guiding what we are going to be doing. I was really happy that I was able to work so closely with Bekah [Walker]. She took it on the next year after I left, and she did the same thing with the current leader when she was guiding the group.

Because of the short stay of many LSJ group members, Walker said that a primary objective of LSJ is to create lasting partnerships and get people to maintain maximum interest in participation for the time that they are involved in the group. Doing this, she said, allows LSJ to "lay the seeds for future members to create something that would last while being realistic about what people can commit too."

The group, Walker said, works essentially as an informal committee of the whole with one member, the Chair, leading the meetings:

> When I was [Chair], we would have two meetings a month. [Being Chair meant] making agendas and trying to decide what I thought we needed to discuss at those meetings—forecasting out from events how much time we would need for x, y, and z, and how many people we might need to do different projects. On a daily basis, being Chair was mostly taking in information from people as they gave it to me [...] collating that information together to share with everyone, seeking input, and trying to come to a consensus.

Other LSJ members take responsibility for different areas such as maintaining the group's social media presence, organizing individual fundraisers, or getting in touch with potential partners.

LSJ decided that they would initially focus on holding fundraisers for different organizations. Grogg had previously been with the Peace Corps in Cambodia, and LSJ held their first event to raise money to help build a library in that country. When Walker took over as Chair in 2016, the group expanded these fundraisers to support various local Iowa City groups, including the Center for Worker Justice (https://www.cwjiowa.org/), an organization that advocates for undocumented workers and other laborers in the state. They also have fundraised for out-of-state organizations like New York's Lisa Libraries (https://lisalibraries.org/), which builds small libraries for children in underserved areas. In addition to such fundraising activities, LSJ maintains ongoing collaborative community partnerships where its members volunteer time with different organizations. The group's primary project, which started in 2015 and continues to the present, is a creative group at a local halfway house that was inspired by Grogg's work with the prison book club. During halfway house events, LSJ members guide residents through different creative activities such as writing exercises, building comics and zines, and listening to and reflecting upon pieces of music. It is SLJ's intent to keep these meetings open in terms of the variety of content provided and format used to allow residents to participate in something different from what most of their other group work is like. Walker said that this project remains one of her favorites to come out of the organization because of its popularity and staying power.

Grogg said that it is easy for students to perceive Iowa City as a homogenous community. However, when you get outside of the university campus "you see there are a lot of people represented in the community, and those were the people that we were trying to reach [. . .] I think that it is important to go outside of your bubble within those communities to make sure you are reaching everyone." Seeking out volunteering opportunities is a good way to both gauge and engage with your community. Another way to understand your community, Grogg said, is to ask them directly about who they are through tools such as surveys. LSJ has used community-polling techniques successfully several times. For example, they have distributed surveys prior to fundraisers as way to determine what the proceeds of the fundraisers should go towards. Doing these things will also increase community awareness of your group's existence.

LSJ has had great success connecting with the local community and is now considering expanding the organization to other locales. One of the advantages of working with a primarily student-based membership is that the people who started the group in 2015 have relocated across the US and beyond, and alumni diffusion will facilitate the building and enabling of chapters at other colleges and universities with library and information science programs. Walker said that, by summer 2019, LSJ would ideally have developed an information pack to distribute to those people who might be interested in starting local chapters. The organization is also working to expand its presence far outside of Iowa City by maintaining a robust social media presence on Facebook that is reaching an international audience. The Facebook page, Walker said, is "kind of like an American Libraries Association think tank, but for social justice issues. I have been encouraged by the direction that [the page] is going, a lot of people are talking about things there, which is exciting."

Grogg and Walker have themselves moved away from Iowa City, the former to Washington, DC, and the latter to Rochester, New York. They have left LSJ in the hands of a new crop of SLIS students as well as local library workers. Both of the former Chairs, however, remain involved with the organization, providing it with guidance and mentorship.

Kelly Grogg is a Digital Librarian at PBS Kids, currently living in Washington, DC. Kelly previously worked as the librarian for the US Peace Corps and was the Olson Graduate Research Assistant at the University of Iowa while obtaining her MLIS. She volunteers as a Court Appointed Special Advocate for children in the foster care system and was named a 2019 Emerging Leader by the American Library Association.

Rebekah Walker is the Digital Humanities & Social Sciences Librarian at the Rochester Institute of Technology (RIT) in Rochester, New York. Previously she was the Director of Operations for IDEAL, a curricular design initiative in the University of Iowa's Rhetoric Department. She holds an Master in Library and Information Science and a graduate certificate in Public Digital Humanities from the University of Iowa and serves weekly as a digital literacy volunteer in the Monroe County Library System in New York.

3.8.1 Takeaways

- Explore opportunities for collaboration between library and information workers and library school students. This provides both a space for engaging with a diversity of ideas and opportunities for mentorship.
- Since student-based organizations see quite a bit of turnover within their ranks, make it clear to members that, for the group to be successful, *everyone* should take ownership.

- Encourage group members to seek out volunteering opportunities within the community in order to gauge and understand that community.
- Social media outlets such as Facebook provide the opportunity to extend local discussions worldwide.

3.9 Libraries Without Borders (Bibliotheques Sans Frontieres): with Allister Chang, Former US Executive Director (May 15, 2018) and Adam Echelman, Current US Executive Director (Feb. 7, 2019)

1342 Florida Ave NW, Washington, DC 200009; (203)-241-1723; https://www.librarieswithoutborders.org/

Founded by historian Patrick Weil in 2007, Libraries Without Borders (LWB) is an international non-profit organization that supports and expands access to information in the most vulnerable contexts worldwide. Although LWB started in France, it presently operates national affiliates across the world. The organization is currently working on, or has successfully completed, projects in the Middle East, West Africa, Europe, Australia, Latin America, and the United States; it will soon be in South Asia as well. It collaborates with outside groups (e.g., small businesses and local libraries) and host countries to make headway in its three stated Areas of Intervention: (1) "Humanitarian Emergencies & Post Conflict Situations," (2) "Access to Information, Education & Cultural Resources," and (3) "Entrepreneurship for Social Change" (Libraries Without Borders, n.d). Each of these Areas of Intervention is comprised of different programs and campaigns that aim to empower communities by providing them with necessary information tools, as well as the skills needed to use those tools.

We interviewed two people for this profile, former US Executive Director Allister Chang, who worked for the organization from 2010 to 2018 (he is now a member of LWB's International Board of Directors), and present US Executive Director Adam Echelman, who took over the reins of the US LWB organization from Chang in January 2019. According to Echelman, "The organization is essentially a series of affiliates, so Libraries Without Borders US shares the same mission [as the other national organizations], but we are autonomous for most of our work." Being the Executive Director of the national organization means leading a team of three staff members and doing everything from designing and imagining new projects, fundraising to make those projects happen, managing their implementation, and designing the evaluation processes necessary to determine project effectiveness. The Executive Director, as a result, engages in all of the activities necessary to make the organization's programs skilled and sustainable.

Chang said that the added value of LWB comes from the organization's expertise "in supporting its library partners, and a lot of that support pulls from our team's business, technology, and policy backgrounds" (Chang himself has a master's degree in public policy from the Harvard Kennedy School). He sees the organization's transformative power in the building of such partnerships through the facilitation of the transformative work of its partners:

> Right now [for example] we are working on a new initiative [the Wash and Learn Program] to build out media centers and libraries inside laundromats where people are waiting on average 90 minutes a week, and often in the winter families go more than once a week to wash their clothes when they have more layers [for a similar project, see Library Laundromat League, p.81]. For an initiative like this, it is not the idea itself that is transformative. Chicago Public Library has been doing this work for decades. I think that where we can really add value is in building out these partnerships beyond the one city that this initiative might be working in and make something that is national or international with broader partnerships and models, new business models, new kinds of partnerships, etc. [...] This kind of work, I think, is critical in building the capacity of local librarians, library systems, and library branches, to have them see less risk in testing something like this.

When asked to expand upon LWB's efforts towards alleviating humanitarian emergencies and taking part in disaster relief efforts, Chang said that this Area of Intervention began to solidify during its 2010 Haiti project. That project began as a partnership with the University Library of the University of Haiti to improve the Haitian citizens' access to information. When US LWB first started the project, they were working through how to improve book donations and pull from best practices to query community members about what texts they wanted before collecting those texts, shipping them, and developing the supply chain of those donations. This was prosaic, if necessary logistical work. According to Chang:

> We were seeing that texts were being shipped in cardboard boxes, which if you were sending them somewhere that might not have a paved road, they will likely get wet and moldy during transportation. Once it arrives it might not

have storage, security, or the cataloging capacity thought through. So thinking about how we collect only the texts that were requested by our local partners and then bringing those to these more isolated contexts more thoughtfully was how we started.

Chang said, however, that "It came as a devastating shock when the earthquake hit," i.e., the earthquake being the 2010 disaster that devastated Haiti and resulted in the death of well over 100,000 people (some estimates put the final death toll at over 300,000). At first LWB considered delaying the project and returning to it when its partners were ready to continue. These same partners, however, asked them to stay and help in the rebuilding process. According to Chang, "it is in that process [of working to rebuild] that we saw how important libraries are in disaster relief as a center for collaboration, as a reference center. It amplifies the capacity of all of the different aid organizations that are working there locally to rebuild." Since the Haiti project, LWB has worked in multiple other disaster and war-torn locations, having a presence, for instance, in Burundian refugee camps serving people recovering from years of civil war, as well as Jordan, Iran, and Europe helping victims of the Syrian conflict.

One of LWB's main activities in disaster-affected areas is the installation of IDEAS boxes. Each box is a self-contained, mobile media center and library shown to provide "educational and psychosocial benefits that improve the quality of life of all refugees" (Hayes, 2016, p. 239). LWB designs the boxes in cooperation with people locally. The organization only goes where is has been invited by local community organizations, and they always customize the content and curriculum of services with organizations that are already working locally. Particular contexts help to dictate the ways in which the IDEAS boxes are used. For instance, when working with Syrian refugees, LWB placed a premium on providing basic information literacy and access to resources. While in West Africa, the context allowed for more opportunities than basic education alone. The refugee camp in Burundi, for instance, offered LWB the opportunity to promote its goal of Entrepreneurship for Social Change, i.e., for the participants of its programs to build out their own organizations, products, and services from the library space. The organization actively works to curate the content within those spaces to foster that particular kind of impact. Per Chang:

You know, entrepreneurship is defined in many ways. My favorite example that comes to mind is... In Burundi where we had the IDEAS box, we had what I

would call cultural entrepreneurs who not only use the library to access infor-
mation, but also use the tools to create and share information and stories. So
create their own movie, edit it using the digital technology provided, and have
the opportunity to share those films at human rights film festivals around the
world. That is one example. Or [as another example] connecting with Etsy style
platforms for products that they are already creating and going through work-
shops on how to find new outlets for their merchandise.

One core belief that extends beyond individual location and IDEAS
box installation is that the library is a space that should be inclusive and
welcoming to everyone. Echelman noted that LWB's projects are
designed to be used by all within that space:

We are setting up for different IDEAS boxes in Bangladesh in an area that has
a really high density of Rohingya refugees from Myanmar Burma. But this is
not a camp per se. It is a community. So, while our programming serves the
Rohingya population, it does not exclusively serve them. We serve everybody
that lives there, and that includes native residents who have lived there for dec-
ades as well as Rohingya refugees. We really want the library to be a space
where people can come together and not a space that is divisive and serves
one community over another.

As one can see from the above description, the LWB Area of
Intervention Access to Information, Education & Cultural Resources is
necessarily tightly interwoven with the other two Areas discussed. Chang,
however, wants to make clear the distinction between "access" and
"accessibility," and the necessity of the latter for the former to be effective. The two concepts, he said,

[...] are very different, one is technical and the other is quite dynamic. The bar-
riers for folks to access existing information are not always technical. A lot of it
has to do with the ways in which information access points are designed, and
designed inclusively. Has it been curated in ways that are relevant and provide
relevant and reliable information? If you provide texts in the wrong language,
offer programs when people are busiest and cannot attend, offer programs
that are hard to get to and do not think through transportation [...] I do not
think those programs are accessible even if they are available. More and more
librarians and our library partners are working with us as creative designers of
information access programs and not just providers of information tools.

Echelman said that US LWB's mission is the same as the international
organization. The work, however, is not so much to replicate what is
happening internationally, but rather to make sure that the US organization hones in on what is relevant and what is appropriate within the US
context. US LWB spends a lot of time thinking about spaces and

communities that libraries simply do not have the capacity and/or the time or the infrastructure to serve. For example, they have been establishing services in spaces like laundromats, churches, and bus stations. The national organization's largest current portfolio is the aforementioned Wash and Learn program, a national effort to bring libraries and librarians into local laundromats through the creation of pop up information spaces. Echelman said that

> What has been so exciting about Wash and Learn has been the ways in which we have been able to build national momentum. In 2017 we formed the Laundry and Literacy Coalition with the Coin Laundry Association and Too Small to Fail, which is the early childhood branch of the Clinton Foundation. Together we started to think about what the national appeal of this program was. So, the Wash and Learn program, for context, is a local effort that we coordinate with libraries. But what we realized through the Coin Laundry Association, and through Too Small to Fail and the Clinton Foundation was that this was even bigger than libraries. Then we started to make a national call to every laundromat owner in the country to say, "we want you to participate."

US LWB also started a Legal Literacy Initiative as a way to think beyond the spaces that people are working in and about the skills that library workers have and the ways that library workers can be leveraged to serve the needs of low-income families in the US.

When queried about the future of US LWB, Echelman said that his biggest goal is to continue to create what he calls "pipeline program to policy." He explained that successful programs like Wash and Learn should be long-term commitments to the community, possibly spanning several decades in order to foster trust. To accomplish this objective, LWB must draw upon the organization members' inherent strengths as researchers, trainers, and coalition builders. When asked if he had any tips for people who might be interested in performing work similar to that of LWB, Echelman suggested that they foster an attitude of "scrappiness" and bring that approach to their work. Such determination means more than simply being innovative; it is a willingness to take action and an innate flexibility that gets things accomplished. Scrappy is also a good adjective to describe LWB as an organization. It is a nimble organization that thinks beyond traditional institutional barriers to information access and accessibility, and it transforms library work in the process.

Allister Chang works to expand access to reliable information. He is currently a Fellow at Voqal and an Affiliate at Harvard University's

Berkman-Klein Center for Internet and Society. Allister served as the Executive Director of Libraries Without Borders from 2014 to 2019, and currently serves on its Board of Directors. He holds a master's in Public Policy from the Harvard Kennedy School, where he was elected President of the Student Government, and a B.A. in History (*summa cum laude*) from Tufts University. He is on the International Literacy Association's 2019 "30 Under 30" List.

Adam Echelman is the Executive Director for Libraries Without Borders, where he works around the US to ensure that all people have access to quality information, knowledge, and culture. His work includes the Wash and Learn Initiative, which brings library services and programs into local laundromats, and the Legal Literacy Initiative, which unites public libraries and legal libraries to serve immigrant families. Adam is passionate about inclusivity and is fluent in French, Spanish, and Chinese.

3.9.1 Takeaways

- Clearly define your organization's objectives and goals. Design them to be complementary.
- Think beyond simply providing access to address issues of accessibility.
- Consider all of your possible constituencies when designing services.
- The library extends far beyond the physical structure of the building. Provide access and accessibility to the people where they live and need it.
- Stay scrappy!

3.10 Library Freedom Project: with Alison Macrina Founder (May 5, 2018)

http://Libraryfreedom.org

US government subcontractor Eric Snowden made his startling revelations concerning numerous government global surveillance programs. The extent of this surveillance was shocking, and it alarmed many library and information workers that conscientiously ascribed to the *American Library Association Code of Ethics'* (American Library Association, 2008) commission to "protect each library user's right to privacy and confidentiality with respect to information sought or received and resources consulted, borrowed, acquired or transmitted." Fortunately, however, the Snowden revelations galvanized the resolve of many of these same library and information workers, encouraging them to take action in support of their patrons.

When the Snowden affair happened, Library Freedom Project (LFP) founder Alison Macrina was working at a public library in Watertown, Massachusetts. She said that she had become a librarian because she saw it as an interesting and challenging field. . .

> But, if I am being honest, I think that the real reason may be a little bit more cynical. I had kind of a Lloyd Dobler [from the movie] Say Anything feeling, like that I did not want to make anything that was bought or sold, and I did not want to do anything exploitative. I did not want to do anything that compromised my far left political views. I tried to make a list of what was out there and there was not much. I think a less cynical way of saying that is that librarianship is one of the only professions that I know of that affords the possibility to do work that is socially important without exploiting the people that you are trying to help.

Macrina was not new to social and political activism. For instance, she been involved with Palestinian justice initiatives during high school. The NSA leak, however, as well as contemporaneous events such as the beginnings of the Black Lives Matter movement and the ongoing concerns surrounding the USA PATRIOT Act, helped her see how she could combine her activism with her library work to effect social change surrounding the issue of privacy rights. Starting out by teaching some privacy classes, Macrina began down the path to what in 2014 would become LFP, a non-profit organization devoted to fighting for patron privacy rights and against systems of oppression using education and action. In 2015, LFP received a grant from the John S. and James L. Knight Foundation, allowing Macrina to leave public library work to run the organization full-time.

There has long been a tension between cybersecurity and personal privacy in the library environment. Ironically, technology is sometimes used to invade privacy in a place closely associated with democracy and personal freedom (Kim, 2016). Bayle et al. (2017) wrote that "some of the main concerns for librarians are how they protect the personal information of their patrons, as well as how they can assist their patron's right to free access to information" (p. 13). LFP speaks plainly when articulating its staunchly anti-authoritarian aims in the face of the creeping surveillance state, as well as the library and library worker's duties in the face of this increasing supervision on the part of government and Big Data. The organization's website states, "We refuse to allow governments and corporations to control our personal data. Librarians can resist the surveillance state and help bring privacy back to their local communities. We can help" (Library Freedom Project, n.d.). It provides this help through a number of different initiatives, with a primary focus being on professional education and training concerning privacy issues and the related responsibilities of today's library and information workers. Macrina said that,

> The main thing that I have been doing for the last few years is traveling to different libraries, library conferences, staff events, things like that, and teaching workshops about privacy. Sometimes I bring a lawyer with me. Sometimes I bring an activist from the American Civil Liberties Union or someone like that. We cover things [during LFP programs] that are happening with privacy. For example, something that we would cover right now would be the Cambridge Analytica story, so whatever is happening in the news that people need to know about. We use it to frame the privacy conversation more broadly. With Cambridge Analytica, for example, you can use that to talk about any kind of surveillance capitalism, as Shoshana Zuboff coined the term. You can talk about what the police are using and what other government agencies use. And then we cover practical things that we can do: strategies for helping patrons, technology, different practices, and things like that.

Currently, Macrina leads approximately 30 of these instructional sessions per year, workshops centering on technology related issues such as the effective use of privacy software, anonymous Web browsers, and search engine technologies. In addition, LFP has online privacy classes for kids, courses about mobile device privacy, and it provides an online toolkit for library workers interested in learning more about privacy issues. Macrina also works with libraries to set up their own anonymous Tor relays, an Internet technology that uses a browser designed to conceal its users' personal information and protect privacy. LFP made national news in 2015 when Macrina provided privacy training sessions to workers at Kilton Public Library in Lebanon, New Hampshire. In the face of adverse government pressure, Kilton would go on to become the first public library in the U.S. to offer anonymous Web access to their patrons using Tor. Because of this success and growing visibility, LFP began receiving an increase of requests for help from libraries across the country (Carollo & Uchell, 2015). The organization's reach is now becoming international, helping Mozilla with its US and Europe-based Glass Room Experience, which curates interactive exhibits about living in an increasingly digital world. It is not surprising that, as the only full-time employee of LFP,

Macrina is constantly working. When she is not having conversations with people about privacy and their libraries, giving advice, consulting and talking with people who want to do workshops, preparing workshops, and giving workshops, she spends a great deal of time working to fund initiatives, doing research about the field, going to conferences, and reading relevant literature.

When asked about challenges that the LFP faces, Macrina said that a primary obstacle she encounters is the tendency of many libraries to shy away from taking actions with political implications. This has left LFP in a strange position where,

> On the one hand, we get a lot of support in the library world where people are excited about us and we have a good reputation, but at the same time there is a lot of risk aversion to doing anything that seems political. So, even though people really want privacy stuff—there is a lot of support and interest and it seems like it is really the moment for this to be happening, a lot of library administrations are really hesitant to do any work with us because they are just afraid.

This reticence on the part of the library as an institution points to larger philosophical issues encountered in library work. Macrina said that library workers should really do some soul searching about their roles in modern society, suggesting that they refer back to their core values and try to live them as fully and carefully as possible. For her, two of the most important of these core values are privacy and access, and "in a world where the internet is increasingly mediated by a handful of private companies for exchanging our personal data, libraries can be a place where you can have access to materials without sacrificing your privacy."

Fortunately, challenging and changing ingrained institutional diffidence sits squarely in LFP's educational wheelhouse. Looking towards the uncertain future of the library, a powerful institution imbedded in societies that seem increasingly bent on actively surveilling their citizens, LFP has recently started the Library Freedom Institute (LFI) in partnership with New York University. This intensive six-month training program—conducted primarily online from June to November every year—introduces and engages a select group of library and information workers with LFP's work. Graduates of the program leave with "the skills necessary to thrive as Privacy Advocates; from educating community members, installing privacy software, to influencing public policy" (Library Freedom Institute, 2017).

One of Macrina's future goals is to take some of these LFI graduates—Privacy Advocates who do not want to just bring privacy into their own libraries but who might want to work with her directly—and transform LFP into something with greater reach and impact. Ideally, she said, "I would like to turn the Library Freedom Project into a cooperative and ask George Soros for something like a million dollars, which is not actually a joke because the reason the right wing goes after him so much is because he is the only one that gives that much money." The growing public consciousness surrounding surveillance and privacy rights, as well as the conversation building about these things, suggests that both LFP and LFI are well-situated as vanguard organizations to effect such instrumental change.

Alison Macrina is a librarian, Internet activist, founder and Director of Library Freedom Project, and a core contributor to The Tor Project. She is passionate about connecting issues of privacy and surveillance to other global struggles for justice.

3.10.1 Takeaways

- Consider how your particular professional interests and skill sets may help to inform and focus your social justice activism.
- What starts as part-time activism has the potential to grow quickly into a full-time job. Do not be surprised when you shift career paths due to this growth.
- A great way to further the type of work that you do is to *teach the type of work that you do* as part of that work.

3.11 National Coalition Against Censorship: With Abena Hutchful, Director of the NCAC Youth Free Expression Program (June 22, 2018)

19 Fulton Street, Suite 407, New York, NY 10038; (212)-807-6222; ncac@ncac.org

In 1974, the New York City-based National Coalition Against Censorship (NCAC) started in response to United States legislature and court attempts to suppress sexually related materials and regulate sexual expression. The 1973 court case *Miller v. California* was a defining moment that led to the Supreme Court redefining its interpretation of obscenity, narrowing its definition of the offense from that which is "utterly without socially redeeming value" to that which lacks "serious literary, artistic, political, or scientific value" (Finkelman & Urofsky, 2003). Through the 1970s, NCAC comprised a coalition of 50 independent organizations, but has since increased its membership to include 57 organizations representing literature, arts, education, and civil liberties (National Coalition Against Censorship, 2019b); groups that have banded together to fight censorship in all its forms through protest and political speech. Abena Hutchful, human rights lawyer and coordinator of NCAC's Youth Free Expression Program (YFEP), told us just how critical this sort of advocacy is:

> When there is a major First Amendment controversy in the national discourse, like the NFL Protests [i.e., where football players knelt during the US national anthem] or March for Our Lives, [NCAC] is helping people understand their rights and the limitations of the First Amendment so that we are having an informed dialogue about it on a national scale.

NCAC has two central initiatives, YFEP and the Arts Advocacy Program (AAP). YFEP mentors and educates students on why and how to assert their freedom of speech rights, providing them with the necessary critical thinking skills. The program promotes young people's participation in the local, national, and global conversations that affect their lives, conducting workshops and school visits to inform students and educators on topics of censorship and free speech. (National Coalition Against Censorship, 2019c). Hutchful said that the program also does significant work with teachers and administrators, assisting them in responding to community requests to censor material in schools. One such collaboration with the National Council for Teachers of English, for instance, develops and distributes resources to dispel censorship myths. When school is in session, Hutchful receives daily censorship reports. She keeps a vigilant eye out for instances of school censorship involving the Internet, books, movies, and music, and she develops resources to counter the lack of information.

AAP aids artists, curators, and art institutions in responding to censorship controversies over artwork. It is the only national project dedicated to working with these groups directly by helping them resolve censorship disputes. NCAC takes a special interest in these cases because artists many times see their rights infringed upon, such as their work being censored when deemed unpopular or controversial. Hutchful said, "We work with artists and curators long term to help them craft the language for responding to censorship in their communities, [and] how to have those difficult conversations in their very sensitive and highly subjective space." AAP helps to resolve these issues through advocacy, policy-making, and educational programs for affected communities (National Coalition Against Censorship, 2019a). NCAC also works with libraries and library workers. Many censorship cases, Hutchful said, begin in the library with community reactions to books and artwork.

On top of these programs, NCAC strives to inform public officials about challenges to the First Amendment. The project collaborates with other free speech groups and civil liberties organizations as part of the Free Expression Network (https://ncac.org/free-expression-network), meeting regularly with allies to organize efforts to influence policy and legislation. The network also works closely with federal employees to fight against censorship and, most recently, the repeal of net neutrality protections.

NCAC serves all communities, including K–12 public and private schools. Hutchful explained the organization's motivation behind serving the younger generations, "We recognize that the students whose voices are often targeted, or who are most vulnerable to censorship, are students of color, queer students, and just students who do not conform with the prevailing ideology of their community." When choosing censorship cases to oppose, NCAC selects those that have broader implications. For example, if attempts at censorship affect one student, the organization assesses how the rights of students in surrounding communities might be infringed upon. Recently NCAC has been focusing more on Internet censorship. Although students' online presence is increasing, the digital divide remains a major problem in low-income areas. In such communities, NCAC actively responds to censorship efforts to filter Internet browsing or abridge access to library materials.

NCAC does not litigate or offer legal counsel, but instead utilizes its members' expertise as lawyers to help others understand the nuances of law. For instance, NCAC has worked with teachers and library workers in high profile textbook censorship controversies. In 2017, NCAC and several other groups urged Rick Scott, the Governor of Florida, to defeat a proposed, and ultimately successful, bill which would give Floridians more power to object to classroom materials and textbooks deemed objectionable, increasing the potential for censorship in the state's K–12 educational settings (Postal & Travis, 2017). School, textbook censorship, Hutchful said, is a major challenge for the organization.

We live in a polarizing, politically charged environment that sometimes negates objective facts and pedagogical value in favor of political indoctrination.

NCAC's limited resources prevent it from being able to reach everyone that its nine-person staff would hope too. Hutchful also suspects that there is some ideological resistance to a New York City-based organization participating in local community work outside of the city. The organization, as a result, must continue to build its credibility to extend their reach. She described their strategy to work closer with communities and grassroots organizations,

> We take the relationships that we build very seriously. We try to work as much as possible with teachers, grassroots organizations, and parent groups so that the advocacy is being seen as coming first and foremost from within the community. We also try to leverage support on social media as much as possible so [our] efforts to advocate for a controversial idea, or just to promote respect for that idea, are not seen as coming from just our singular voice, but from the broader community.

Moving forward, NCAC seeks to continue engaging communities in difficult dialogues. Hutchful described the country as divided into ideological bubbles that many times provoke contentious discourse. In the face of such rancor, NCAC encourages civic discourse and engagement that empowers artists, students, and educators, in turn making them champions for freedom of speech. They hope that by offering training and resources, people can overcome the fear of punishment and state their opinions even in the face of vehement opposition. The organization's goal, Hutchful said, is to encourage more people to be comfortable with being uncomfortable.

Abena Hutchful is a human rights lawyer and advocate. Prior to joining the National Coalition for Censorship (NCAC), she worked on United Nations projects in post-conflict settings, getting people access to education, devising campaigns to combat xenophobia, and promoting local integration. After working in the Sudan and witnessing its harsh repression of the press, civic life, and freedom of expression, Hutchful became interested in how information affects the public welfare of the American people. She came to the NCAC to grow its Youth Free Expression Program, engage and mentor youth, and work with school administrators and teachers to promote civic participation and free expression.

3.11.1 Takeaways

- Social justice organizations tend to be relatively small. Forming coalitions provide strength in numbers.
- Facilitating dialogue to educate on freedom of speech can help individuals stand up for their opinions, even in a polarizing environment.
- Work as much as possible with teachers, grassroots organizations, and parent groups so that advocacy is seen as coming from within the community.
- Leverage support on social media as much as possible so your efforts to advocate for a controversial idea are not seen as coming from just a singular voice.

3.12 Progressionista: with Shanel Adams, Founder (July 10, 2018)

P.O. Box Detroit, MI 48235 USA; http://www.progressionista.org

Detroit Michigan is in the midst of a literacy crisis. It has been reported and frequently repeated that up to 47% of the city's adults are functionally illiterate (National Institute for Literacy, 1998). Although the reliability of that statistic has been disputed, there remains little doubt that many of the city's young people face great adversity. Detroit's public schools have reported exceptionally low proficiency scores in literacy (Laird, 2017), and students and their parents encounter barriers to education including "safety issues, lack of transportation, and lack of information" (Lake, Jochim, & DeArmond, 2015, p. 23). The poor state of public education in Detroit has even led to a lawsuit, *Gary B. v. Snyder (2016)*, where the plaintiffs argued that the Detroit school system has denied them a fundamental right to literacy (although the case has been dismissed by a federal judge, it is currently under appeal). At a basic level, literacy is a social justice issue involving the distribution of educational and economic opportunity as well as the distribution of power that these opportunities entail. With Detroit's majority African American population, estimated at 79.1% (United States Census Bureau, n.d.), it becomes difficult to conclude other than that race is a factor in the denial of opportunity through basic education, whether done premeditatedly or not. Organizations like Detroit's Progressionista, however, are working to redress such institutional deficiencies and inequalities by providing alternative avenues to literacy and self-actualization that celebrate community, identity, and culture. Although it is still a young organization, Progressionista is a valuable model for other educational initiatives seeking to fix the structural failings of educational institutions through positive action. It accomplishes this task through the written word's power to inspire, as well as the power of role models to galvanize girls' self-esteem and drive.

Shanel Adams, a writer, communications professional, and current graduate student in library and information science at Wayne State University, started Progressionista in 2014 after graduating from college and moving back to her home town of Detroit. Adams has always had a love for libraries and books—she came up with the idea for Progressionista while at the public library—and envisioned the book club as a space "where the girls can read exciting books and meet phenomenal women;" she herself having met many such women when in college. From September through May, Adams and other Progressionista workers meet once a month with a small group of pre-teen, school age girls. All of the participants are minorities, all are from the inner city, and most are African Americans. Currently, 15 girls take part in the program, and it is the same group of girls for the entire school year. Adams wants the girls

> [. . .] to see that literature can change the way that they think, and that they can discover themselves through it. That is my story. I learned a lot from books. I read to find out anything about or to identify with women. I want girls to see all of these phenomenal women and know that they can read their way to where [such women] are.

It is not surprising, therefore, when Adams cites maverick children's author Roald Dahl as an inspiration for what she has accomplished. She appreciates how Dahl interpreted children as being their own people, and pointed to one of his quotes that sums up the scope of her own efforts with Progressionista: "I have a passion for teaching kids to become readers, to become comfortable with books, not daunted. Books shouldn't be daunting, they should be funny, exciting and wonderful; and learning to be a reader should give a terrific advantage" (Dahl, 2010, p. 85).

To accomplish this task, to gain this advantage, the young participants meet monthly with a local woman professional (a "progressionista"). Every school year, Progressionista provides an array of such speakers, women that come from a range of backgrounds and represent a variety of different careers, both white and blue collar, and have included a dentist, an engineer, a dancer, and a bus driver. Adams pairs the encounter with a book to read and discuss, and each month's selection relates in some way to the speaker's professional life:

> We will have a dentist come. Then we read a book related to her field. It is always a fiction book. The book when the dentist came was a graphic novel called Smile [by Raina Telgemeier (2010)]. It is really popular amongst kids. And then the best part about it is that the girls get to do hands on activities. So, when the dentist came we taught them how to do molars and do some dental exams on each other.

During another recent meeting, the girls met with a local baker, heard her story, and decorated their own little cakes. The book that went along with the fun was *Cupcake cousins: Summer showers* (2015), by Kate Hannigan and Brooke Boynton Hughes. All of these activities, however, are done with three outcomes in mind, i.e., to "Double the leisure reading time of participants," to "Expose participants to local women professionals," and to "Increase participants' reading by at least one grade level" (Progressionista, n.d.). As a result of these commitments, the organization works towards self-empowerment through both encouraging reading and exposing participants to the stories of role models who also attribute some measure of their own success to a love of reading. Progressionista's accomplishments, borne out by its growing ability to attract participants as well as the recent opening of a second, Chicago-based Progressionista group, provides additional confirmation of its success.

Nonetheless, there have been obstacles along the way. For Adams, a major challenge has been securing buy-in from parents. Such buy-in is important because it determines whether the parents want their kids to give the program a try, as well as ensures their girls' regular attendance. Adams said she at first tailored everything that she did towards interesting the girls and making sure that they were having fun, but attendance remained low. When she switched her approach to include communication and marketing to the parents, participation increased:

> The interest increased because the moms determine a lot of how the kids perceive things. So, we started doing little things, like raffles and gifts for the moms. Little things to include them in it so they were excited to bring their daughter. I think that just having buy-in from the parents, or just community members at large, helps with moving anything you forward because they are the ones you want to show up.

When asked to suggest tips for those educators and activists beginning similar projects, Adams noted the importance of doggedly hunting for outside support. She spends a good deal of her time securing outside partners and suggested that anyone beginning similar projects should make certain that they are constantly considering people and organizations that they might be able partner with. Such outside help need not be monetary:

> For me it is not just the professional speakers [to ask to take part in programs], but also organizations. I can go to see if they have any women that they suggest for our programs. One organization that we work with a lot is First Book [https://firstbook.org/]. They always give away free books, so that is another opportunity that we use. And for me personally, it is also making sure that I have a good relationship with the librarians at our [public] library [where Progressionista meets] because they basically run the whole library. That is very important as well.

Adams' persistence has paid off. Interest in the program has led to a boost in participation both in terms of community support as well as in the number of girls wanting to take part in the book club. The increase in interest has Adams thinking about how to best move forward while maintaining the intimate nature of the groups. When she had 20 girls attending during a school year, it did not feel the same as when she had 15 or less taking part, and she does not want to lose that sense of intimacy. At the same time, Adams feels that the more girls that Progressionista reaches the better, and exclusivity would run counter to the program's purpose. Her goal, therefore, is to build a structure that allows the organization to duplicate Progressionista into additional small groups in both Detroit and elsewhere: "The Chicago group has definitely been a learning experience for me by teaching me how to do that. I do not know how, like what the time table will be on how I will be able to have a ton of chapters or anything, but I do think that is the model that I am going for."

Progressionista is a young and energetic organization, and this energy runs in stark contradistinction to the perceived stagnancy of Detroit's public schools. This is a counter-hegemonic organization in the most fundamental sense, working as a counterpoint and corrective to an educational system that stifles learning because of its inherent structure and burdensome bureaucracy.

Shanel Adams is the founder and Director of Progressionista, a library-based book club program for girls where they meet a woman professional at each meeting. She founded Progressionista in 2014 after attending Howard University and realizing how much leisure reading as a child impacted her life. Shanel is currently a library services graduate student at Wayne State University's School of Information Science.

3.12.1 Takeaways

- Community buy in is an important factor in increasing participation and project visibility. Be creative in your marketing and public relations strategies to get people excited.
- Partner with outside organizations. Carefully consider the ways in which they can benefit your project, monetarily and otherwise.
- Small can be better. Aim to maintain the intimate nature of a project even when expanding. Consider way to expand your project while maintaining such intimacy.

3.13 Street Books: with Laura Moulton, Founder (May 21, 2018)

PO Box 13642 Portland, OR 97213; http://streetbooks.org/; librarian@streetbooks.org

Although library services are typically associated with the library as a physical place, recent years have seen an increase in the number of services that subvert this notion by expanding the concept of library far outside of the building (or foregoing the building altogether) to better serve underserved and at risk populations that might not have easy access to services. One such effort is the "books on bikes" type program that delivers the library directly to the people where they live. Some of these programs are outreach initiatives run by local library systems. One of the earliest such efforts, for example, being the Seattle Public Libraries' Books on Bikes Program (Bales, 2018). Other projects, like Portland Oregon's Street Books, work entirely outside of the traditional public library system.

In 2011, Laura Moulton started Street Books, a non-profit street library that provides those experiencing homelessness with access to books by way of two bicycle-driven book carts. She derived inspiration for the program in part from an art project and in part from a conversation. Moulton is an adjunct college professor and artist that works in the medium of social practice, a participatory art form that involves community members directly in the art-making process. In 2010, she initiated a project at Portland State University in which she constructed a mobile rolling gallery, the Object Mobile, featuring Portland State University students' precious objects (Moulton, n.d.). This art exhibit, which encouraged community member interaction and active participation, was, Moulton said, a "sort of the run up to the Street Books idea." The conversation that helped to mold the project happened on the streets of Portland with Quiet Joe, a man that lived outside by choice:

> He and I had a conversation one day just standing on a curb about books that we liked. He told me that one of his favorite authors was A.B. Guthrie, who wrote The Big Sky, and it kind of blew my mind because I had grown up in rural Idaho reading those same books. I like A.B. Guthrie, and I was struck that day by the fact that we had books in common. I think that lit a little candle in the part of my brain about what other assumptions I had had about people living outside and what they might be up for in terms of a participatory project.

In 2011, Moulton commissioned her brother to help her build a rolling library—a tricycle with a plywood book box on the front—and Street Books started business.

The homeless population is a heterogeneous one coming from a variety of backgrounds and having different information needs (Hersberger, 2005), and Street Books serves a wide range of people currently experiencing homelessness. Borrowers include men, women, and occasionally teenagers, children, and families. Patrons often live in encampments of tents or cardboard structures, while others live out of their cars. Some people may even choose to live on the street. A number of people living outside may be in treatment for drug addiction and/or may suffer from mental illness. In recent years, Moulton has observed a level of suffering that she had not previously encountered. Portland is in the midst of a housing shortage, leading to a rise in the number of homeless encampments. Compounding the problem, there has also been an increase in the availability and affordability of hard street drugs. She said that the unpredictable nature of working outside, combined with the general lack of similar organizations to serve as exemplars, has required Street Books to carefully consider operating procedure:

> There are not many street libraries like Street Books that focus specifically on our demographic, on our population. As a result, we have had to build a street

librarian protocol. For example, rules and regulations when operating the bike in the city. That has been an interesting challenge, to make sure that we create a system that works for everybody, that is safe for the librarians. I do not want to imperil the librarians or put them into a position where they are vulnerable.

Since beginning in 2011, Street Bikes has expanded to two bike libraries and now employs six to eight part-time street librarians, several of whom have experienced homelessness themselves. A street librarian's typical day consists of loading the book cart up with about 50 titles curated to include a diverse blend of fiction and non-fiction books and then heading to several different locations across the city where people congregate. One regular stop is the Portland Martin Luther King Jr. Worker Center, which is designed for workers, many of whom are Spanish speaking, who might not be able to access employment through traditional means. The street librarian sets up the library, displays the books (for the Worker Center, its offerings include many Spanish language selections), and, depending on how lively the traffic is, remains onsite from an hour to an hour and a half. The street librarian maintains a consistent schedule so that the patrons know where to return a book and check out a new one. The circulation system is an old-school card-in-pocket system, and while returning books is suggested, it is not required. Although many borrowers have gone to great extremes to get items back to the carts, life outside can be especially hard on books. They can be stolen, and patron's situations are changeable, leaving them unable to get the items back. The street librarians invite borrowers to bring the book back in a week or so, but if their path does not cross with Street Books again, patrons are encouraged to pass the book on to somebody else that will enjoy it. Moulton remembered one particular patron,

> *[...] a kid who was just passing through. He was going to hop a train going towards the Rainbow Gathering, and he was longingly looking at a Jack Kerouac book. He said, "Man, I would love to take this, but I just don't know when I am coming back through Portland, and I don't know if I can find you." I said "dude, take this book. If you are going to take a train, you need On the road." So, we operate much more in terms of matching a person with a book. That takes precedence over worrying about stock. We can always get more donations.*

Moulton maintains the operating principle that "no matter where a person is sleeping, I think that there is always a book that can be at the center of a conversation." This philosophy is refreshing, and particularly so when one considers the US public library's historically troubled relationship with homeless populations. While there are many great public library outreach programs to the homeless and traditional library workers that "understand what cuts in federal assistance for housing programs and social services mean to the people they serve" (Gieskes, 2009, p. 56), there are also those institutions and library workers that view people experiencing homelessness as a "disruptive population" (Hersberger, 2005). Funding for such library outreach programs to the homeless, furthermore, may be limited or non-existent. Public libraries also often lack the infrastructure or training necessary to serve people living outside. By working outside of the system and by employing only people passionate and invested in helping this underrepresented population, Street Books does away with the bureaucracy and focuses entirely on filling the need. Considering that Street Books employs several former homeless people among its street librarians—approximately half the organization's 2018 crew have experienced homeless—the organization possesses another advantage over public libraries where the homeless are often effectively "segregated for special attention" (Holt & Holt, 2010, p. 111). These street librarians are intimately aware of the diversity of the population as well as the diversity of their information needs, something that handicaps public library initiatives that might inadequately understand this heterogeneity and persist in "thinking in terms of 'the homeless' as an archetypal example" (Muggleton, 2013, p. 17).

Although Moulton would prefer that Street Books be made obsolete due to a lack of need, the program is expanding, both internally and by way of example. Portland winters can be unforgiving, and Street Books work shifts have sometimes been canceled because of rain and cold. As a result, they effectively operate as a street library only from June through October. The organization, however, has recently opened an onsite library and headquarters in an affordable housing project where approximately 30% of the residents are recently transitioned from the streets. The three to four hundred book onsite collection, Moulton said, "has been great because it allows us to be able to continue the programming through the winter months." She has also had a number of people contact her who are interested in starting similar projects in their own countries and in their own cities. Most recently, for example, Moulton heard from organizers working in Brazil. In addition, Street Books has a recent sister library in Austin Texas, Street Books Austin (Street Books ATX, n.d.), and it is Moulton's hope that people can create similar projects that involve outreach to communities that our vulnerable and/or underrepresented.

Laura Moulton is the founder of Street Books, a bicycle-powered mobile library that serves people who live outside in Portland, Oregon, (http://streetbooks.org). She has taught writing in public schools, prisons, and teen shelters, and is an adjunct professor at Marylhurst University and Lewis & Clark College. Her social practice art projects have included postal workers, immigrants, prisoners and students. She has received an award from the National Book Foundation, as well as an Excellence in Teaching award from Marylhurst University. Her MFA is from Eastern Washington University.

3.13.1 Takeaways

- Look to what you love to do, even if it might seem like it falls outside of the scope of library and information work, as possible inspiration for your progressive library and information projects.
- Carefully consider establishing sound operational protocols to ensure the safety of your employees and/or volunteers in non-traditional environments.
- Remember that old technology may be perfectly functional for your project's needs, as well as more affordable.
- Avoid treating the populations that you serve as one-dimensional entities. Venture out into the community, become a part of that community, and get help from that community.

3.14 Whole Person Librarianship: with Sara Zettervall, Founding Consultant and Trainer (Nov. 6, 2018)

https://wholepersonlibrarianship.com/

Whole Person Librarianship (WPL) is the brainchild of Sara K. Zettervall, a public librarian in the Minneapolis area, and Mary C. Nienow, a professor of social work at St. Catherine University in St. Paul, Minnesota. We spoke with Zettervall about this unique initiative that recognizes and supports the evolving dialectic between library work and social work.

Before starting WPL, Zettervall had worked with professional social workers while employed at the University of Minnesota's Center for Early Education and Development. Drawn to public library work, she then went to library school at St. Kate's University in St. Paul. Her experiences at St. Kate's were eye opening:

I was not even familiar with the term social justice until I went into library school. That is where I really started to learn what it meant. I think a real turning point occurred when I did an internship where I went to juvenile detention facilities and some other places where they were doing outreach work, and realized that it was a real passion for me to provide library services to people from a variety of different backgrounds. I really wanted to do solidly community-based library work.

Zettervall followed this internship with a library school practicum where she worked with a book club for teen Somali girls. During this experience, she once again connected with social workers, co-leading book club sessions with WPL co-founder Nienow. The two discussed what each other did professionally and, Zettervall said,

I felt like many of the things that I learned from her about the way that social workers approach communities and the people that they worked with were applicable to what I needed to know in order to do the kind of library work that I wanted to do. That was where the idea of Whole Person Librarianship first came from, and it has evolved over time as the interest in libraries doing collaborative work with social workers has grown in these last few years.

Billing itself as "The Hub for Library-Social Work Collaboration" (Whole Person Librarianship, n.d.), WPL began in 2012 as a professional blog exploring such partnerships between library workers and social workers. While feedback was initially slow, Zettervall said that response to the blog began to build momentum. Library workers and social workers found the website, and became interested in what Zettervall and Nienow were doing. People intrigued by the blog also began asking Zettervall to present at conferences on the connection of library work and social work. Because of this response, WPL's mission "has shifted to educate librarians and library staff on relevant social work concepts and tools" (Zettervall, n.d.).

Westbrook (2015) wrote, "Today's tensions between librarianship and social work have their roots in professional debates that were well underway at the dawn of the last century. Initially centered on libraries' role in acculturating immigrants, these conversations continued regarding services for World War I veterans, poverty-stricken families of the Depression, and World War II veterans becoming first –generation college graduates" (p. 7). Libraries have employed professional social workers for some time now, with the San Francisco Public Library being the first to hire a dedicated social worker in 2009. This hiring, Zettervall said, came in response to the large number of patrons experiencing homelessness who were using the library essentially as a day shelter, many bringing with them concerns like mental health issues and drug addiction. Following San Francisco's lead, other public libraries in cities like Denver, Washington, DC, and Edmonton began hiring social workers as a connection point to their homeless populations.

The presence of social workers at public libraries, Zettervall said, made visible the need for social work related training among library staff, and such instruction is something that libraries can incorporate beyond the limits of solely having to hire specialized personnel. Zettervall offers training sessions to libraries and other organizations that seek to incorporate ideas drawn from the theory and practice of social work into their operations, educating on topics like how library staff set boundaries or understand trauma informed care approaches to patron services. She has engaged in a number of sessions in different formats:

> I have done some webinars. I have been asked to come and give in-person trainings in various places. The longest training that I did was a daylong training for the staff of a collaborative of rural librarians in Michigan that was starting an Institute of Museum and Library Services grant. They had hired a social worker to come in, and they wanted their library staff to have a strong grounding and understanding of some of those basic social work concepts in order to be able to work with them. Next year I am going to do a couple of in-person trainings for the State Library of North Carolina. A cool thing that I have coming up is a webinar with the State Library of Victoria in Australia. That is exciting to get it spreading worldwide. I am also starting a professional development online course.

The above quotation demonstrates that WPL's work is spreading beyond the public library milieu to engage other audiences. Zettervall is seeing growing interest from university and community college libraries, particularly places where the library workers observe some of these needs in students coming into the library for help, and whose institutions may not have as robust student services as other places. Social work graduate programs have also expressed interest in what WPL offers.

Zettervall said that the WPL website has transformed from a blog into a place to connect folks who are involved in all different aspects of library/social work collaboration. Library employed social workers, for example, will recommend the site to their colleagues recently hired by libraries and suggest that they join the WPL email list. Master of Social Work students doing internships have used the website to connect with each other. It is a place where people bring their questions and share the projects that they are working on. This is a valuable tool, Zettervall said, because people doing this type of work have started small and may feel isolated. After seeing the increasing number of conference presentations and programs devoted to the intersection of library and social work, she added an event calendar to the website that functions as a communication point, providing people a place to share notice of any presentations, conference sessions, or online instruction opportunities that focus on the library-social work collaboration.

Zettervall and Nienow started with a novel idea and stuck with it because they saw things that people needed and then responded to those things. When asked how WPL developed its program, Zettervall said that she has learned that success involves building connections and fostering relationships; one should not try to go it alone. She also recounted an interview she conducted for a recently published book coauthored with Nienow, *Whole Person Librarianship: A social work approach to patron services* (Zettervall & Nienow, 2019). The interviewee likened putting together their social work collaboration to "building the plane while they are flying it." Running WPL has been much like this; it is about identifying gaps and needs over time, registering what people are asking from the organization and carefully considering how to fill those needs. Zettervall stressed the need for similar projects to remain open to all possibilities, and continue to evolve organically where the need is:

> My motivation is to make sure that we do not lose sight of the fact that this work is broader than just one particular place. There is a lot of interest out there, a lot of interest beyond just the model that grew out of San Francisco having that full-time social worker in a big urban library.

Looking to the future, Zettervall has considered merging WPL with a professional organization such as the Public Library Association, but said doing so would likely address only one segment of interest in the need that is out there. Part of the reason, she said, that WPL remains an independent space is that, since it operates at the juncture of two different professions,

> There is no easy answer to say, "This is the professional home" in terms of professional associations. There is no easy way to say, "This is where we need to be." There is no single place with a low enough barrier on entry that is going

to meet the needs of everyone who is interested in this and want to learn about it. We are grappling with that now.

Zettervall pointed to the website *Programming Librarian* as an aspirational model for WPL. It is a site that originated in a similar way, i.e., as the creation of people responding to a need which has developed into a focal point for collaboration and a respected entity independent from any professional organization. WPL is an idea that is constantly unfolding; a project that finds strength in professional collaboration and cross-pollination.

Sara K. Zettervall, MLIS, MFA, is the founding consultant and trainer at Whole Person Librarianship. She instructs library staff across the nation and the world on applying social work concepts to improve library service. She and social work professor Mary C. Nienow co-authored the first book on library-social work collaboration, *Whole Person Librarianship: A social work approach to patron services* (Libraries Unlimited, August 2019). Sara has served in the American Library Association for many years, beginning as a LLAMA-sponsored 2014 ALA Emerging Leader and continuing to her current involvement in the Equity, Diversity, and Inclusion Task Force Recommendations Implementation Working Group. She has published on outreach and social justice in *Public Libraries*, *VOYA*, *American Libraries*, *Library Youth Outreach*, and *Progressive Librarian*.

3.14.1 Takeaways

- Break silos by working and dialoguing with professionals outside of library and information work.
- There are advantages to remaining an independent organization and space. You may tailor what you offer to more than one audience.
- Ideas and projects inevitably change. Stay open to all possibilities and evolve organically.

References

American Civil Liberties Union. (2019b). *PFLAG V. CAMDENTON R-III SCHOOL DISTRICT.* Retrieved from https://www.aclu.org/cases/pflag-v-camdenton-r-iii-school-district.

American Library Association. (2008). Professional ethics. Retrieved from http://www.ala.org/tools/ethics.

American Library Association. (2014). Access to library resources and services to minors: An interpretation of the Library Bill or Rights. Retrieved from http://www.ala.org/advocacy/intfreedom/librarybill/interpretations/access-library-resources-for-minors.

American Library Association. (2019). Prisoner's right to read: An interpretation of the Library Bill of Rights. Retrieved from http://www.ala.org/advocacy/intfreedom/ librarybill/interpretations/prisonersrightoread#Notes.

Antigone Books v. Brnovich, 2:14-cv-02100 (2015).

ATD Fourth World. (n.d.). Our mission. Retrieved from http://www.atd-fourthworld. org/who-we-are/mission/.

Awesome Foundation. (n.d.-a). About Us. Retrieved from https://www.awesomefounda tion.org/en/about_us.

Awesome Foundation. (n.d.-b.). Libraries. Retrieved from https://www.awesomefounda tion.org/en/chapters/libraries

Bales, S. (2018). *Social justice and library work: A guide to theory and practice*. Cambridge, MA: Chandos Publishing.

Bayle, E., Compoe, S., Ehrick, R., Hubbell, D., Lowe, B., & Ridge, J. (2017). Patron privacy: Is the Tor browser right for library use. *Computers in Libraries, 27*(6), 10−13.

Braithwaite, J. (2002). *Restorative justice and responsive regulation*. Oxford: Oxford University Press.

Carollo, M. & Uchell, J. (2015, Sep. 17). How a small New Hampshire library stirred up a digital rights debate. *The Christian Science Monitor*, Retrieved from https://www. csmonitor.com/World/Passcode/2015/0917/How-a-small-New-Hampshire-library-stirred-up-a-digital-rights-debate.

Chmara, T. (2017, June 26). 20 years of online free speech. Retrieved from https://www. oif.ala.org/oif/?p = 10180.

CNN Wire. (2014). Ferguson's "School of Peace." *Fox 2 Now St. Louis*. Retrieved from https://fox2now.com/2014/08/23/fergusons-school-of-peace/.

Dahl, R. (2010). *The missing golden ticket and other splendiferous secrets*. New York, NY: Puffin Books.

Doe v. Gonzales, 386 F. Supp. 2d 66 (D.Conn. 2005).

Finkelman, P., & Urofsky, M. I. (2003). *Miller v. California. Landmark decisions of the United States Supreme Court. Washington, DC.* CQ Press. Retrieved from http://library. cqpress.com/scc/lndmrk03-113-6441-348249.

Freedom to Read Foundation. (2019a). About FTRF. Retrieved from https://www.ftrf. org/page/About.

Freedom to Read Foundation. (2019b). Judith Krug Fund Education Project. Retrieved from https://www.ftrf.org/page/Krug_Education.

Gary B. v. Snyder, Civil Action No.: 16-CV-13292, (2016).

Gieskes, L. (2009). Why librarians matter to poor People. *Public Library Quarterly, 28*, 49−57.

Hannigan, K., & Hughes, B. B. (2015). *Cupcake cousins 2: Summer showers*. Los Angeles, CA: Disney/Hyperion Books.

Hayes, A. (2016). Thinking outside the (Ideas) box: Education as life-saving aid during protracted refugee situations. *Alexandria, 26*(3), 235−242.

Hersberger, J. (2005). The homeless and information needs and services. *Reference & User Services Quarterly, 44*(3), 199−202.

Holt, L. E., & Holt, G. E. (2010). *Public library services for the poor: Doing all we can.* Chicago: American Library Association.

Inklebarger, T. (2014). Ferguson's safe haven. *American Libraries, 45*(11/12), 17−18.

Kelley, J. (2013, June 18). Judith Platt, Sen. Russell Feingold win 2013 FTRF Roll of Honor Awards. Retrieved from http://www.ala.org/news/press-releases/2013/06/ judith-platt-sen-russell-feingold-win-2013-ftrf-roll-honor-awards.

Kemshall, H. (2008). Risks, rights and justice: Understanding and responding to youth risk. *Youth Justice, 8*(1), 21−37.

Kim, B. (2016). Cybersecurity and digital surveillance versus usability and privacy: Why libraries need to advocate for online privacy. *C&RL News, 77*(9), 442–451.

Laird, L. (2017). Right to learn: Advocates for Detroit students say there is a constitutional claim to literacy. Retrieved from http://www.abajournal.com/magazine/article/constitutional_right_to_learn

Lake, R. J., Jochim, A., & DeArmond, M. (2015). Fixing Detroit's broken school system. *Education Next, 15*(1), 20–27.

Larue, J. (2007). *New inquisition: Understanding and managing intellectual freedom challenges.* Westport, CT: Libraries Unlimited.

Librarians for Social Justice. (n.d.). Librarians for Social Justice. Retrieved from https://www.slis.uiowa.edu/current-students/lsj.

Libraries Without Borders. (n.d.) Our activities. Retrieved from https://www.libraries-withoutborders.org/activities/.

Library Freedom Institute. (2017). Application Questions + Details. Retrieved from https://libraryfreedom.org/wp-content/uploads/2017/12/LFI-Application-Questions-121017.pdf.

Library Freedom Project. (n.d.) We fight surveillance. Retrieved from https://libraryfreedomproject.org/.

Media Coalition. (2019). Antigone Books v. Brnovich. Retrieved from http://mediacoalition.org/antigone-books-v-brnovich/.

Miller, R. T. (2015). The heart of service. *Library Journal, 140*(11), 8.

Miller v. California, 413 US15 (1973).

Moulton, L. (n.d.). Object permanence. Retrieved from http://www.lauramoulton.org/object-permanence/.

Muggleton, T. H. (2013). Public libraries and difficulties with targeting the homeless. *Library Review, 62*(1/2), 7–18.

National Coalition Against Censorship. (2019b). The coalition. Retrieved from https://ncac.org/project/arts-advocacy-program.

National Coaltion Against Censorship. (2019a). Arts advocacy program. Retrieved from https://ncac.org/project/arts-advocacy-program.

National Coaltion Against Censorship. (2019c). Youth free expression program. Retrieved from https://ncac.org/project/youth-free-expression-program.

National Institute for Literacy. (1998). *The state of literacy in America: Estimates at the local, state, and national levels.* Washington, DC: Government Printing Office.

Postal, L. & Travis, S. (2017, April 20). Parents may get say on books bill broadens who can ban texts in schools. Sun Sentinel (Fort Lauderdale, FL), p. 1.

Prison Policy Institute. (2018). Youth confinement: The whole pie. Retrieved from https://www.prisonpolicy.org/reports/youth2018.html.

Progressionista. (n.d.). About Progressionista. Retrieved from https://www.progressionista.org/about.html.

Project NIA. (n.d.). About Project NIA. Retrieved from http://www.project-nia.org/.

Reno v. American Civil Liberties Union, 521 U.S. 844 (1997).

Salter, J. (2014, August 10). *Protesters rally after black teen's shooting.* Associated Press News Service.

Street Books ATX. (n.d.). About. Retrieved from https://streetbooksatx.wordpress.com/about/.

Sweeney, P. (2018). Building political support for your library through surfacing. *Journal of Library Administration, 58*(8), 873–880.

Telgemeier, R. (2010). *Smile.* New York, NY: Graphix.

Westbrook, L. (2015). "I'm not a social worker": An information service model for working with patrons in crisis. *Library Quarterly, 85*(1), 6–25.

Whole Person Librarianship. (n.d.). Welcome. Retrieved from https://wholepersonlibrar-ianship.com/.

Young, M. V., Phillips, R. S., & Nasir, N. S. (2010). Schooling in a youth prison. *Journal of Correctional Education*, 61(3), 203–222.

Zettervall, S. (n.d.). About. Retrieved from https://wholepersonlibrarianship.com/about-2/.

Zettervall, S., & Nienow, M. (2019). *Whole person librarianship: A social work approach to patron services*. Santa Barbara, CA: Libraries Unlimited.

Further reading

American Civil Liberties Union. (2019a). America's addiction to youth incarceration: State by state. Retrieved from https://www.aclu.org/issues/juvenile-justice/youth-incarceration/americas-addiction-juvenile-incarceration-state-state.

Library Freedom Project. (n.d.-a) Library Freedom Institute. Retrieved from https://library freedomproject.org/lfi/.

PFLAG v. Camdenton R-III School District, 853 F. Supp.2d 888 (2012).

United Stated Census Bureau. (n.d.). *Quick facts: Detroit city, Michigan*. Retrieved from https://www.census.gov/quickfacts/fact/table/detroitcitymichigan,mi/PST045217.

CHAPTER FOUR

Connect and transmit: organizations for professional support and outlets for professional communication

4.1 Introduction

The final five profiles in this book are for projects through which transformative library and information workers are able to establish professional or intellectual connections with each other:

1. Allied Media Conference: Radical Libraries, Archives, & Museums Track
2. Feminist Task Force of the American Library Association Social Responsibilities Round Table
3. Joint Conference of Librarians of Color
4. Rainbow Round Table
5. Urban Librarians Conference

Three of the profiles—Radical Libraries, Archives, & Museums Track, Joint Conference of Librarians of Color, and Urban Librarians Conference—cover library and information science related professional conferences that focus on issues surrounding progressive, radical, and transformative library work. The other two projects—Feminist Task Force and Rainbow Round Table—are both American Library Association membership groups that support the interests of both at-risk patron populations and at-risk library workers.

The five profiles here are an admittedly small group. Many other groups and projects, such as EIFL: Electronic Information (https://www.eifl.net/) and Information for Social Change (http://libr.org/isc/), would also serve as excellent models for anyone considering beginning a social justice related effort. The profiles we do provide, nonetheless, are fine representatives of the ongoing efforts within the information professions to encourage solidarity through active organization, representation, and dialogue.

Transformative Library and Information Work.
DOI: https://doi.org/10.1016/B978-0-08-103011-0.00004-6 © 2020 Elsevier Ltd.
All rights reserved. 123

4.2 Allied Media Conference: Radical Libraries, Archives, and Museums Track: with Andrea Perez, Co-Founder and Past Organizer (Oct. 16, 2018), and Katie Dover-Taylor, Co-Founder and Past Organizer (Oct. 19, 2018)

https://www.alliedmedia.org/amc2017/rad-libraries-archives-museums-track

The Allied Media Conference (AMC) was started as the Midwest Zine Conference in 1999 by Jason Kucsma and Jen Angel, former editors of *Clamor* magazine, and received its current name in 2002. Now under the auspices of the Detroit-based Allied Media Projects (AMP) (https://www.alliedmedia.org/), AMC is an annual event that "explores the intersections of media and communications, art, technology, education, and social justice" (Allied Media Projects, n.d.-a). The conference brings together community organizers, technologists, writers, filmmakers, and other people involved with media to learn, network, and share about participatory media-based organizing, i.e., "any collaborative process that uses media, art, or technology to address the roots of problems and advances holistic solutions towards a more just and creative world" (Allied Media Projects, n.d.-c). Media formats represented at the conference have included everything from radio broadcasting, to zines, to graffiti.

The diverse programming at AMP includes Network Gatherings, Practice Spaces, and Tracks. Network Gatherings are day-long events for groups to do "strategic planning, media-making, and other activities that support their year-round organizing and collaboration," Practice Spaces feature hands on activities like makerspaces and pop-up media shops, and Tracks are 90 minutes sessions "held together by a shared theme" that include events like workshops, presentations, and performances (Allied Media Projects, n.d.-b, p. 8). Recent Tracks have included "Magic as Resistance," "Healing Justice," and "Movement Journalism" (Allied Media Projects, n.d-a), and participants are not limited to attending any one Track. In 2015, AMC debuted the Radical Librarianship Track, which was renamed the Radical Libraries, Archives, and Museums Track (RadLAM) in 2017. RadLAM gives participants the opportunity to "learn how to use collections, knowledge, programs, and services to support social justice work, empower the public, amplify marginalized voices, and build a better world" (Allied Media Projects, n.d.-d).

Two Westland, Michigan public library workers, Andrea Perez (who has since left Westland Public Library to become a therapist and a public librarian in the Detroit suburbs) and Katie Dover-Taylor (Reference Librarian and Web Content Coordinator at Westland Public Library), initiated what is now RadLAM. Perez told us that at the time of the Track's formulation in late 2014, they had become largely disengaged with the American Library Association (ALA) and the Public Library Association (PLA):

> I just did not feel like I got much from [the ALA and PLA conferences] or the state association conference that we had. So I was hoping for something that could bring together librarians and archivists, and professionals and practitioners along with students. Something that could bring them in close contact with the public, because at ALA and all of our professional conferences we are just talking to ourselves alone in these silos.

Perez approached Dover-Taylor with the idea of starting an AMC Track relating social justice, libraries, and library work. The latter was intrigued by the idea, seeing it as fitting well into her own praxis, and feeling that "what [was already happening] at this conference seems to me to be the work of librarianship writ large and done by people who do not consider themselves librarians. I was like 'Let's get in on that.'" A Track for progressive library workers would do much to further integrate information workers (many of whom had already been attending AMC) into the conference milieu, as well as provide additional opportunities for learning and engagement to other conference-goers regardless of their areas of expertise.

Indeed, Perez and Dover-Taylor envisioned the Track as a means for developing solidarity and supporting coaction both within the library community and between progressive library workers and the larger activist community. Attending the conference and Track would allow library workers who might feel marginalized within the profession to connect with likeminded colleagues and, as a result, gain the sense that they are not alone in their social justice work. Second, the Track would provide a space for library workers to escape the echo chamber of their traditional LIS conferences by bringing them into contact with a diverse group of activists and organizers from outside of the discipline. Not only would the library worker be able to learn new activist and organizational skills to incorporate into their own praxis, they would have the opportunity to dialogue directly with non-library workers about library and information related issues during RadLAM sessions. In fact, some of the best conversations at the conference, Perez said, were those held in sessions attended by non-library workers: "We can guess what the public wants, but when we can actually talk to them, it takes [the dialogue] to a whole different level." Non-librarians may also propose and deliver RadLAM sessions, further strengthening connections between activists of diverse backgrounds and breaking down traditional disciplinary, organizational, or institutional silos. Session titles from the 2018 RadLAM schedule illustrate the broad range of topics covered, their potential appeal to a wide variety of different types of activists, and the practical, hands-on spirit of the conference (Allied Media Programs, n.d.-d):

- "Hacking Wikipedia: How to bring your community to the world,"
- "791.4 HYPE Radio — Teen Podcasting in the Library,"
- "Today's Equity: Tomorrow's Museum,"
- "Libraries Empower Incarcerated Youth," and
- "Fringe Issue: Sex Work & Night Life Organizing."

Both Perez and Dover-Taylor were new to activism and conference organizing when they proposed the Track. This was not much of an obstacle, however, because AMC is run both by and for community organizers and activists, regardless of experience level. Perez said that first-time Track coordinators find AMP a great organization to work with because the organization has been doing the conference for so long. Dover-Taylor reiterated this point, that

> The cool thing about the conference is that the AMC staff provide the infrastructure. They make sure we have a location, and there is food for people, and they take care of all the logistical coordinating. But then the stuff about the contents is sort of peeled off and done in a more democratic way where the folks who are coordinating have a series of milestones. We have to call for proposals for our Track. We receive those proposals. We make suggestions about what would be in the final content of our Track. The final decision [on content] is done by the AMC staff who have a lot of experience creating the conference. Then we fundraise to help bring presenters to the conference and get the word out about the Track. And then for us, we felt there was an important piece in making sure that the presenters felt taken care of during the conference. We assigned ourselves to go to different sessions and deal with any last minute things that were needed.

The conference is tightly coordinated and executed. AMC has developed excellent processes for approving its Tracks as well as for preparing Track coordinators for the event. Coordinators submit proposals in

November for the June conference held in the following year. They then follow a timeline in which they propose Track subjects as well as basic outlining for what they would cover. After the AMC staff select Tracks, Practice Spaces, and Network Gatherings for the conference, the organization bring in those who have had their proposals accepted for a crash course in organizing the conference and session finalization. Every year, AMC also publishes a set of fantastic zines about how the conference is organized   (https://www.alliedmedia.org/news/2016/03/15/read-our-newly-updated-amc-zines-2016). Activists and organizers will find these publications valuable reads regardless of whether or not they are planning for AMC.

Despite the great amount of help provided by AMC staff, coordinating RadLAM is quite a challenge. Dover-Taylor said that those doing similar work should be prepared to work with many different people to get things done and be prepared to navigate personality differences, disagreements, and hurt feelings. Burnout is also a real possibility. After the 2016 conference Perez and Dover-Taylor decided that, even though both would remain engaged in the Track, it was time to hand over their coordinator role to others. Dover-Taylor said that

> That transition from finishing the first year [2015]—since the conference is in June—and then having to propose in November of the same year for the next year's conference was exhausting. I was burned out and was like "I can't put all of this energy into this right now." But I was really glad that other people had responded to [the Track] and responded to it enough that they wanted to keep it going. That was cool!

The two cofounders, however, had set up RadLAM to succeed. Both the Track and AMC have been hugely successful. Conference attendance has increased so much over the past several years that AMP declared 2019 to be "A Year in Chrysalis," meaning that there will be no conference that summer, and they will spend the year, developing "the new shapes the AMC can take to support [its] networks brilliant media-based organizing" (Allied Media Projects, n.d.-a). Likewise, and just four years into the game, RadLAM now attracts participants from across the USA and from many different library environments, including public, academic, and school media centers, providing a space for collaboration, cross-pollination, and solidarity.

Andrea Perez (she/they) is a social worker and librarian currently living in the metro Detroit area. They were one of the co-creators of the

Radical Librarianship track at the Allied Media Conference in 2015. Andrea worked in public libraries for over 11 years before going back to school to obtain a master's in social work from Wayne State University. They now work as both a mental health therapist and as a public librarian.

Katie Dover-Taylor (she/her) is a public librarian, organizer, and fifth generation Detroiter. In 2015, Katie was a founding co-coordinator of the Radical Librarianship track at the Allied Media Conference in Detroit. She is particularly interested in the theory and practice of anti-racist librarianship, especially in the public library setting. She is member of the PLA Task Force on Equity, Diversity, Inclusion and Social Justice.

4.2.1 Takeaways

- Look for opportunities to break out of disciplinary, organizational, or institutional silos and echo chambers. Learn from knowledge allies coming from outside of library work. Share your knowledge with them.
- Experienced activists and organizers, even those operating largely outside of progressive and radical library and information work, are often willing to share their expertise with newbies. Seek them out.
- Be prepared to work with many different personalities and to wind up in conflicts. Cultivate patience and empathy.
- Transformative library and information work can be overwhelming. Work hard to get things running, but know when it is time to take a break and hand the reins to someone else.

4.3 Feminist Task Force of the American Libraries Association Social Responsibilites Round Table: with Sherre Harrington, Task Force Coordinator (Oct. 4, 2018)

50 E. Huron St. Chicago IL 60611; (800)-545-2433; http://www. ala.org/rt/srrt/feminist-task-force

Following the first wave of feminism of the early 1900s, the 1960s again saw issues of gender come to the forefront in a turbulent period that included "protests, riots, demonstrations, and assassinations" (Hildenbrand, 2000, p. 53). Women library professionals had already been shouldering the past with little recognition: histories of influential female library workers being sparse and infrequent, and men retained the majority of positions of power within the field. Furthermore, as McElroy (2017) observed, "Feminists have long recognized both that women's work tends to be underpaid, and that women often do additional work on top of whatever they're being paid for" (p. 89). The time had arrived to demand equality and fairness in library work, and the upsurge in library work-related feminist activism was greatly bolstered in 1970 with the creation of what would become the ALA SRRT Feminist Task Force (FTF) (Hildenbrand, 2000).

FTF is a sub-unit of the Social Responsibilities Round Table (SRRT) of the American Library Association (ALA), an organization that represents library workers and information professionals interested in the intersection of library work and social justice. FTF has gone through several name changes since 1970, starting out as the Status of Women in Libraries, becoming the Task Force on Women later that decade, and switching to its current moniker in 1980 (Cassell, 1980; September). Over the past 50 years, FTF encompassed many different areas of advocacy, including equal rights and pay for women and sexism in the library workplace. Sherre Harrington, the task force's current Coordinator, said that the organization has evolved through the years:

> [FTF] is a fluid group founded on feminist practice. The idea being that [the task force] is a place to come if you have something you want to be done. If you have an idea, if you have a project, Feminist Task Force can support that within ALA to give you a foundation, a platform, a home for the sort of things that you might want to accomplish.

From its beginning, social activism and the promotion of women's rights has always been a core element in of the group's activities, and this component extends to direct action. For example, in 2017, Breanne Butler, Evvie Harmon, and Fontaine Pearson organized the Women's March, a protest designed to encourage women from across diverse communities to educate, demonstrate, and promote equality and human rights for all women (Women's March, 2019). That same year, the ALA Midwinter Conference was held in Atlanta, Georgia, and FTF was one of several ALA groups that encouraged the organization to get members involved in the Atlanta March for Social Justice and Women. Approximately 200 librarians from ALA Midwinter participated in the march (Eberhart, 2017; January 21). Harrington said that creating a sense of community among members by engaging in social activism together, and not alone, was a unifying moment.

As part of ALA, FTF regularly contributes programming to the parent organization's annual conference. Starting in 1970 with a focus on the status of women library workers and the Equal Rights Amendment, FTF has featured academics like Anita Schiller, Pauline Iacono, and Kay Cassell as speakers (Kagan, 2015). Over the years, conference events have included panels, speaking sessions, and celebratory functions. It has since sponsored sessions and workshops on topics such as "sexism in librarianship, women and political clout, pornography and censorship, and racism and ethnic diversity in librarianship" (Feminist Task Force, 2005). The task force also frequently holds author events at ALA Annual, and has had many such events over the years, bringing in notable feminist authors such as Dorothy Allison, Jules Gomes, and Susie Bright. In 2017, for instance, Kelly Jenson, former librarian and editor of the book *Here we are: feminism for the real world* (2017), moderated a panel of cutting-edge feminist authors featuring writers Mikki Kendall, Erika L. Sanchez, Brandy Colbert, and library worker Jessica Pryde (Harrington, 2017).

FTF's recent programming has centered on women in media. At the 2018 ALA Annual Conference, it cosponsored a community Wikipedia Edit-a-thon with the Association of College and Research Libraries, Women and Gender Studies Section titled *Women of Library History Wikipedia Edit-a-thon I, II, & III (SRRT)*. This event encouraged participants to create Wikipedia entries for women who have influenced and advanced libraries and library work. In the process, the Edit-a-thon connected attendees with the larger Wikipedia library worker community as well as presented them with valuable resources to continue editing in their individual area of expertise (Harrington, 2018).

In an effort to reach a younger audience, FTF curates an annual list of feminist books for children and young adults with its well-received Amelia Bloomer Project (https://ameliabloomer.wordpress.com/), named after Shanna Corey's (2000) book, *You forgot your skirt, Amelia Bloomer!* In the spirit of Corey's book, FTF convenes an annual committee to recommend titles that are well written and illustrated, that feature strong female protagonists, call out or help to eliminate sexism, solve problems and blaze new trails for women, break stereotypical bonds of society, and empower others (Amelia Bloomer Project, n.d.). Once the committee selects a calendar year's titles for inclusion, they categorize them by age group and post the list online for the benefit of library selectors.

Fleming and McBride (2017) wrote that, "Cultivating safe spaces in the profession is essential. Safe spaces allow us to express our frustrations and celebrations without fear of being misunderstood" (p. 119). FTF was founded on these principles, creating a space where women can come together, without judgment, and they will continue to do so. Harrington seeks to gain a more prominent media presence for the task force as FTF shares their programs and mission with new and potential members. She wants the task force to continue supporting the feminist agenda, providing free information to both members and non-members alike who are interested in issues related to women and information. As task force leadership turns over, Harrington said that creating and maintaining a robust online presence is essential to grow the organization's member base. In support of such a presence, FTF digitizes and makes available its newsletters online, as well as heavily promotes task force initiatives through their Facebook page. As FTF moves forward, they will continue to explore initiatives that advance women's interests in the library world such as providing travel scholarships to members traveling to ALA conferences or small grants for research and projects supporting a feminist agenda.

FTF will hold its 50th anniversary celebration at the ALA 2020 Annual Conference. The once feminist minority in library work is slowly becoming a feminist majority, demonstrating the task force's influence. As Harrington noted, "There are feminists everywhere. You do not have to go to a special room for it anymore."

Sherre Harrington obtained her Master of Library Science degree from the University of South Carolina (USC) and is currently the Director of Berry College's Memorial Library in Rome, Georgia. In the late 1980s, Harrington became involved with the Feminist Task Force. She credits her passion to advocate for feminism to many people that she met along her path to and during librarianship, women with strong careers, but also strong feminists. One mentor in particular, Sue Rosser, former Director of Women's Studies at USC, gave her many opportunities to make the connection between librarianship and the bigger world, taking her experiences beyond the closed culture of information professionals.

4.3.1 Takeaways

- An essential element of feminist praxis is community. One must promote each other and advocate together, rather than alone.

- Feminism and library work are a natural fit, sharing basic elements. They both support the free access to resources and education in support of diverse communities.
- Creating and maintaining a robust online presence is essential to grow a project's member base.

4.4 Joint Conference of Librarians of Color: with Kenneth A. Yamashita, President of the Joint Council of Librarians of Color (Nov. 7, 2018)

P. O. Box 71644, Los Angeles, CA 90017-0644; https://www.jclcinc.org/

The Joint Conference of Librarians of Color (JCLC) was the idea of Satia Marshall Orange, former Director of the American Library Association (ALA) Office for Literacy and Outreach Services (OLOS) and is a home for those who work to support communities with the library resources and services necessary to enhance their constituents' access to information. Following Orange's appointment as OLOS Director in 1997, she convened an informal dinner at 1998 ALA Midwinter that included leadership from five ALA ethnic affiliates: the American Indian Library Association, the Asian/Pacific American Librarians Association, the Black Caucus of the American Library Association, the Chinese American Librarians Association, and REFORMA: The National Association to Promote Library & Information Services to Latinos and the Spanish-Speaking. At this dinner and subsequent conversations, Orange discussed the idea of having the five affiliates join forces to stage a joint national conference. The first JCLC took place in 2006 and welcomed, regardless of associational membership status, all who serve and support communities of color, equity, diversity, and inclusion.

Coming to fruition in Dallas, Texas, 2006, the inaugural JCLC was themed, "Gathering at the Waters: Embracing Our Spirits, Telling Our Stories." Each of the five affiliates provided seed money to support the launch, with additional financial support from various contributors (PAG, 2006). The conference program included an open letter welcoming attendees with the following:

> JCLC 2006 is dedicated to improving the quality of communication and information sharing about our issues and communities within the library profession, especially between the five ethnic caucus organizations and their advocates

[. . .] you will find a myriad of ways you can impact your communities and improve the productivity of your library in regards to diversity and multicultural-ism (Bell, 2006).

Programming ranged from sessions with National Public Radio's Juan Williams, human-rights activist Loung Ung, sociologist Bertrice Berry, and activist Mayra Montero, to various sessions "geared to librarians of color as well as those who serve multicultural populations in all types of libraries" (Miller & Bardales, 2006; PAG, 2006, p. 20). The conference was a great success with over 1000 registrants.

JCLC returned in 2012, this time in Kansas City, Missouri. Themed "Gathering at the Waters: Celebrating Stories, Embracing Communities," it attracted over 800 library workers and exhibitors (SinhaRoy, 2012), and it offered sessions on topics such as "advocacy, outreach, multicultural collection development, diversity best practices, recruitment, and delivery of services" (Morales, 2012). Speakers included Emmy Award winning *Sesame Street* actor Sonia Manzano, best-selling youth literature authors Sharon Flake and Lauren Myracle, and adult literature author Julie Otsuka (Figueroa, 2012).

In June 2015, the five affiliates officially incorporated as a non-profit organization, the Joint Council of Librarians of Color, Inc. (hereafter referred to as Joint Council to differentiate it from the conference). Current Joint Council President Kenneth A. Yamashita, explained to us that

One of the primary reasons that we decided to go out and establish ourselves as an incorporated non-profit organization, was that we did not think we could sustain the support of ALA over the long term for JCLC. We decided to incorporate and become our own entity to be the fiscal agent for JCLC. The first thing we realized was that it is really hard work to produce a conference, so we were extremely grateful that ALA provided that support for the first two conferences. [Yet], producing our own conference gives everyone involved a lot of valuable experience in the mechanics of planning and producing the conferences. I think it was very beneficial to the [Joint Council] Board and the Steering Committee—all of whom are volunteers—that we decided to go out on our own.

Joint Council's purpose statement affirms its charge, "To promote librarianship within communities of color, support literacy and the preservation of history and cultural heritage, collaborate on common issues, and to host the Joint Conference of Librarians of Color, 2019" (Joint Council of Librarians of Color, 2019). The non-profit has a five-member Board comprised of one representative from each of the affiliates, and it provides oversight and support for a ten-member conference Steering Committee comprised of two appointees from each affiliate. In 2016, the Joint Council Board decided to host JCLC every four years after the 2018 conference, with the next JCLC in 2022.

The Joint Council Board spent the years leading up to the 2018 JCLC advising and collaborating with the conference Steering Committee to develop and design the event to be held in Albuquerque, New Mexico. The theme for the 2018 conference, "Gathering all Peoples: Embracing Culture & Community," had notable authors Benjamin Alire Sáenz and E. Ethelbert Miller as keynote speakers (Morales, 2018). The conference was a resounding success, with over 1000 attendees registering and over 100 presentations focused on session tracks that included, "bridge building, intersectionality and inclusion, advocacy, outreach and collaboration, technology and innovation, collections, programs and services, and leadership, management, and organizational development" (Kostelecky, 2018). A Scholarships and Awards GALA, "honored individuals selected by each of the five ethnic affiliates to receive JCLC Advocacy Awards, JCLC Distinguished Service Awards, JCLC Author Awards, and JCLC scholarships. In addition, JCLC Legacy Awards and JCLC Rising Leader Awards were presented at the JCLC 2018" (Morales, 2019).

Yamashita said that "after the 2018 conference, we saw how much everyone appreciated our efforts and [how] everyone is looking forward to 2022. We know that the conference had a meaningful impact on all of the attendees." Yamashita told us that the Joint Council Board and the 2022 Steering Committee are planning the next conference's location, registration process, and promotion and advertising, and that he hopes that the Joint Council Board will be able to provide sponsored scholarships in the form of travel awards to attend future conferences. Even though JCLC has followed a rather winding path over the years, it remains true to what its founder Satia Marshall Orange told *American Libraries* in 2006, it is a place where "everybody is somebody... It's not that they're not valued at the other conferences, but it's different when it's your family" (PAG, 2006, p. 34).

Kenneth A. Yamashita is the president of the Joint Council of Librarians of Color. Yamashita earned a Master in Fine Arts from Indiana University. While in school, he worked at the Montclair Public Library, Montclair, New Jersey under the direction and mentorship of Arthur Cooley, former director and past president of the American Library Association. Yamashita next obtained his Master in Library Science from

Rutgers University, followed by a doctorate in library management from Simmons College in 1982. Although he is now retired, Yamashita continues to devote his time and energy to the Joint Council.

4.4.1 Takeaways

- A focused message when working with diverse collaborators and leaders can improve intersectionality and multiculturalism.
- Providing a professional outlet for diversity creates a professional community and compassionate environment.
- Sharing the stories and professional experiences of a diverse population can nurture people of color as informational professionals.

4.5 Rainbow Round Table: with Ana Elisa De Campos Salles, Current Chair (Oct. 18, 2018)

http://www.ala.org/rt/glbtrt

The Rainbow Round Table (RRT) began as the Task Force on Gay Liberation under the aegis of the American Library Association's (ALA) Social Responsibilities Round Table. After adding a sufficient number of members, it gained round table status in 1970 (divisions being ALA's largest member-based groups, followed by round tables, and then task forces). The organization next changed its named to the Gay, Lesbian, Bisexual, and Transgender Round Table (GLBTRT), and, in 2019 became the Rainbow Round Table (RRT). Gay, lesbian, bisexual, and transgender (GLBT) is a historic acronym, but the round table is interested in evolving as new members seek to identify within the organization. Current Chair Ana Elisa de Campos Salles told us that the new name reflects how the round table "is meant to be a place for queer librarians and our allies, and to be a resource for them," i.e., a place to help queer librarians and allies advocate for queer constituencies and to help them provide their patrons resources and services.

RRT is a robust group with 17 standing committees working on various initiatives: updating bylaws, designing webpages, issuing promotion and news updates, and conference programming to name a few. Among the various committees, the Stonewall Book Awards, Rainbow Book List, and Over the Rainbow Book Lists committees engage in a tremendous amount of work promoting access to quality LGBTQIA + (lesbian, gay, bisexual, transgender, pansexual, genderqueer, queer, intersex, agender, asexual, and ally) literature. These three committees form annually to review exceptional English-language books relating to the LGBTQIA + experience published in the United States in the previous year. The Stonewall Book Awards started out as the Gay Book Award and became an official ALA award in 1986. Once selected, RRT presents award winners with $1000 and a commemorative plaque at the ALA Annual Conference. Both the Rainbow Book List Committee and the Over the Rainbow Book List Committee review books and publish annotated bibliographies for select reader populations. The Rainbow Book List Committee selects books for young readers from birth through age 18. The Over the Rainbow Committee considers fiction and non-fiction and publishes a list of age appropriate titles for readers 18 years and older (Socha, 2019). De Campos Salles reflected on why these lists are important resources and how they assist library workers as advocates and allies:

> If [library workers] want to advocate either to their communities outside of the library or to their stakeholders and managers as to why they should have pride displays or how they can go about getting some support internally for what they are trying to do, we are basically here as a resource for them. Our members, of course, are passionate and awesome about wanting to be involved in the round table and in helping to create these resources to be there for each other and to help in the running of the round table itself.

In addition to supporting authors and their work, RRT actively supports new LGBTQIA + library professionals. Recently de Campos Salles initiated a one-on-one round table session for prospective members at the 2019 ALA Midwinter Conference. She theorized that many prospective members are overwhelmed trying to determine which divisions, round tables, and taskforces are right for them and believes an introduction to RRT is necessary. RRT also sponsors an ALA Emerging Leader each year. In the last two years, the round table has managed an Emerging Leaders Project, with the year's Emerging Leader working to improve RRT's archive by organizing it and making it more accessible to members. De Campos Salles described the importance of this historical body of documents, ephemera, and, potentially in the future, oral histories:

> During our 50th anniversary, [the archive] is pertinent. It has always been pertinent, but now would be a nice time to update [the archive] and have something in place accessible online [where] you can see photographs, pamphlets,

old newsletters, tee shirts, and stuff like that. You could also contribute an oral history and be interviewed by the Emerging Leaders about your role in the round table and what it means to you and how it has changed.

De Campos Salles and the board are adding one more component to the archiving project to align with their 50th Anniversary Golden Jubilee celebration set for the 2020 ALA National Conference in Chicago. She proposed, with the board voting, to establish a two-year RRT Archive Project ad hoc Committee to tie up loose ends of the original project. This committee, De Campos Salles said, will be chaired by an "'Emerged Leader'—what those who complete the program are called— with one or two additional Emerged Leaders, as well as RRT members with a variety of relevant skills and backgrounds, including web design, oral histories, and archives." This initiative is on track to assist the 50th Anniversary Golden Jubilee ad hoc Committee with the Chicago festivities, and it will run a photo and memories booth at the celebration where it will exhibit past materials from the archives as well as collect members' memories and stories for the collection.

Honoring efforts to support and advocate for LGBTQIA + causes, communities, or the librarian profession, RRT grants three awards to deserving individuals or groups. The round table's Award for Political Activism honors librarians or library related organizations, library staff, library boards, library friends, and individuals or groups that have performed outstanding contributions and championed LGBTQIA + efforts through activism on a local, statewide, national, or international level (Gay, Lesbian, Bisexual, & Transgender Roundtable, 2019a). The Larry Romans Mentorship Award, named in Romans' honor for his exemplary service in mentoring professionals in the field of librarianship, is a joint award given by the RRT and the ALA Government Documents Round Table. The award recognizes librarians who have made a difference in the profession through ongoing mentoring efforts, thereby encouraging others to serve as mentors and influence the lives and careers of LGBTQIA + library and information workers by helping them succeed in the profession (Gay, Lesbian, Bisexual, & Transgender Roundtable, 2019b). Finally, the Newlen-Symons Award for Excellence in Serving the GLBT Community goes to a librarian, library staff member, library, library board, and/or library friends group that has developed innovative programs and initiatives responsive to the needs of the GLBT community. The award champions individuals or groups that have increased, enhanced, and sustained services to the GLBT community (Gay, Lesbian, Bisexual, & Transgender Roundtable, 2019c).

RRT advocates for human rights causes close to the organization's agenda. For example, when RRT members started advocating for gender-neutral restrooms at conferences, the round table collaborated with ALA to pass a gender-neutral bathroom resolution at the 2018 ALA Annual Conference. RRT is working with ALA Conference Services to develop pamphlets to inform all ALA members of the availability of gender-neutral restrooms at the association's Midwinter and Annual conferences, as well as a second pamphlet to inform conference center employees working about the changes during the event.

De Campos Salles, the RRT board, and their volunteers are preparing for the round table's 50th Anniversary celebration. As RRT moves forward, de Campos Salles has been working to update their bylaws, which have become increasingly outdated as changes have forced the group to evolve quickly to meet the needs imposed by the organization's growth. She has proposed using language that is more inclusive, and the RRT mission statement and by-laws now use the acronym LGBTQIA+ in replacement of the outdated GLBT. The RRT has historically been responsive in the past concerning such issues surrounding language and inclusivity. For example, in 2011, they changed "transgendered" to "transgender" in their name to reflect preferred terminology in the community (Gay, Lesbian, Bisexual, & Transgender Roundtable Newsletter, 2011). De Campos Salles will be working with the Executive Board and Bylaws Committee to usher in future changes, and will update a technically perceptive procedural manual developed under the tenure of a previous chair once the bylaws are brought up to current practices. Fortunately, de Campos Salles has the support of the ALA Office for Diversity Literacy and Outreach Services, and she is working with a staff liaison who assists with questions and advises her on the task force's long-term care and planning.

De Campos Salles takes pride in the fact that she listens carefully to members, and she said that constantly advocating for members and evolving with their needs is necessary to maintain a healthy organization:

> I think it is great that [members] are speaking up and being more vocal because [ALA] has become such a behemoth that people forget this is a membership driven organization. [RRT] needs to keep changing because, if we do not change, we are going to lose new members. If it stops being an organization that speaks to the membership, then we should not be shocked when our numbers start declining.

Ana Elisa Campos Salles works at San Francisco Public Library as the Branch Manager. She received her master's degree in forensic archeology and stumbled into librarianship after applying for a position at her local public library as a library associate, then eventually receiving her master's degree in library science. She is currently the Chair of the American Library Association's Rainbow Round Table.

4.5.1 Takeaways

- A project that fights for underrepresented groups should tailor their advocacy and policy making to include the values and concerns of all their members.
- Highlighting members, persons, and allies within the LGBTQIA + and other historically marginalized communities through awards is essential to bringing their extraordinary contributions to the forefront.
- Transformative projects need to evolve to ensure they are not only meeting current member's needs, but future member's needs.

4.6 Urban Librarians Conference: with Lauren Comito, Founder and Conference Organizer (Oct. 19, 2018)

https://www.urbanlibrariansconference.org/

The New York City-based Urban Librarians Conference (ULCON) is an annual event put on by Urban Librarians Unite (ULU). Since 2013, ULCON has provided a space where urban library workers come together to discuss things that concern them, many of which revolve around social justice related issues. A small but intimate event, the conference is notable for the success of the Do-it-yourself (DIY) approach of its organizers as well as its affordability. During the event, there are three concurrent sessions with a total of around 10 presentations over the course of a single day, as well as a poster session. A sample of presentation titles for their 2019 conference showcases the range of topics covered as well as the importance of justice issues to urban library workers: "Community & Justice for All: Restorative Justice Practices for Public Libraries," "Created by and for People in Need: Use of Community at the Minneapolis Central Library," and "Coming Out Day Screenings and Coffee Chats: Queer Individual Storytelling in an Academic Library Space" (Urban Libraries

Conference, n.d.). Every year there is also a keynote speaker; 2019, for instance, featured sociologist Eric Klinenberg, author of *Palaces for the people: How social infrastructure can help fight inequality, polarization, and the decline of civic life* (2018). There is also a highly anticipated conference after-party where participants can relax and make connections.

We spoke with ULCON organizer Lauren Comito both about the conference as well as about its parent organization ULU. Comito has worked in public libraries for twelve years where she has taken on a variety of roles. She is currently the Neighborhood Library Supervisor at the Leonard Branch of the Brooklyn Public Library. An advocate for urban library workers, she has published many articles on the subject, as well as the books *Grassroots library advocacy* (Comito, Geraci, & Zabriskie, 2012) and *Tech for all: Moving beyond the digital divide* (Comito, 2019). Comito's advocacy work developed out of her library work when, in 2010, hundreds of NYC library workers received layoff notices and had to fight to keep their jobs. Because of the employment situation, Comito cofounded ULU, of which she is the current Chair of its Board of Directors. ULU is a 501c3 non-membership (i.e., you do not have to pay anything to belong) professional organization with an eight person Board of Directors and additional volunteer members coming from New York City (NYC) and surrounding areas of the North Eastern USA. ULU advocates for libraries and library funding in NYC and anywhere else that the organization is invited to help. They have developed a variety of successful projects and initiatives since starting out. ULU provides library workers with training sessions on activism as well as resources such as toolkits for activists. They have created valuable electronic tools for progressive library workers including a database of resources for helping library workers serve refugees and immigrants (Urban Librarians Unite, n.d.-a). They also run a database that keeps up-to-date information on local elected officials (Urban Librarians Unite, n.d.-b). This may be important Comito said,

> if you are at a party and you see someone with the elected official lapel pin you can go through [the database] photos to see who it is, see what committees that person is on, what other issues they care about, and talking points on how to possibly address those issues through libraries. So if they really care about older adults, there would be a little elevator pitch you can give about older adults and libraries.

ULU also serves as an important community connection point for urban library workers, providing opportunities for networking, comradeship, and the exchange of ideas. The organization, for instance, holds popular monthly socials "to give working library professionals and library school students a space to let off steam, network, and share the joys and hardships of our daily work" (Urban Librarians Unite, n.d.-c). ULCON also came about as a means to develop the community of urban library workers, and, Comito said, had been advocating for urban libraries for several years when,

> [...] as I and some of our colleagues were going to conferences, we were notic-
> ing that a lot of the conference programs were not dealing with the things
> that we were dealing with every day. Like how to help patrons who are home-
> less. Like how to deal with the emotional labor that comes from having to help
> people who are poor or homeless try to find housing, but there is no way to
> help them find housing, and then having to go home somehow and still have
> that in your head. And all the programs you were seeing in conferences at the
> time—and I think these events have gotten a lot better over the last couple of
> years—were really things that required a lot of money, or that were from the
> suburban areas that required a larger capital expenditure on their libraries than
> we had. And there was not really anywhere to go for support specifically cen-
> tered on the work we do in urban centers.

In 2013, ULU held the first ULCON to address this gap. The conference is intentionally kept small; about 250 people attend it every year. It
is also purposefully kept inexpensive, with a conference registration currently going for 35 USD (compare this to the cost of many national organizations' conference registration fees, which routinely run into the 100s
of dollars). Since public library workers—a group that makes up the bulk
portion of ULCON's attendees—do not make a lot in wages, Comito
said that, "Keeping the price point at a cost where somebody can schedule themselves a day off and come to the conference without having to
get their employer to pay for it is really important." One strategy that
ULCON's organizers use to keep costs low is to take a DIY approach to
the event. Every year, the three or four conference organizers take on a
heavy workload with some additional volunteer help coming when
needed from ULU board members. The small group keeps registration
materials straight, gets all of the conference materials printed up, and even
brews and makes coffee available throughout the day of the conference
(this last effort is no trivial undertaking; coffee service at a large state and
national conferences can cost hundreds of dollars per urn). All of this labor
takes a level of commitment not often needed with the larger conferences
that have larger organizational capacity. Comito, for example, worked the
day of ULCON's first conference suffering from a severe case of

bronchitis. In addition to their DIY approach, ULCON's organizers seek out sponsorships to keep registration costs low. The Brooklyn Public Library, for instance, donates public library space to hold the event, and the New York and Queens Public Libraries sponsor other parts of the event. When asked how such a small crew keeps up with all of the work necessary to keep things running smoothly, Comito noted the importance of paying careful attention to organization—luckily something library workers tend to be good at—and the value of developing easily updatable spreadsheets. Building and relying on relationships both within and without the library profession has also mitigated the obstacles to ULCON's success:

> Everybody I asked for help from was really helpful. I mean, I spent some four or five years before [ULCON] developing relationships through the advocacy work [...] So we wrote [the idea for ULCON] up and told people "we want to do this." They all said yes. I think it filled a spot that was missing. I think that if you have your stuff organized, you know what you are going to do, and you have an idea that fills a vacant spot in the landscape of professional education, people are willing to help you fill that spot.

Comito sees ULCON as a great "first place" for people to present at, as a space to help develop new library workers and give them an opportunity to speak without necessarily having to spend a thousand dollars or more on travel: "We have had a lot of really good luck with that, and a lot of great presentations from people who were just getting started." ULCON is presently in a good spot. The conference has sold out for the past two years, the presentations they offer address topics of concern to urban library workers, and one does not have to break the bank to attend the event. Comito, however, does not see ULCON expanding in size in the future. Holding the conference in a hotel or renting a space to put on a larger program would likely at least double the price for attendees. Furthermore, one of ULCON's greatest assets is its ability to create solidarity and community from members of NYC's many different neighborhoods, something that massive meetings like those of the American Library Association or the Public Library Association struggle to do. This does not mean that ULU is slowing down or remaining static in their efforts to keep library workers from dialoging about urban library work's unique challenges and issues. For example, the organization will soon be starting up its "Late Night Conversations," a bi-monthly panel series that will be similar in purpose and content to the annual conference.

Lauren Comito is a cape wearing, sword swinging, ukulele playing, tech training, job search helping, activist librarian in NYC. As a Neighborhood Library Supervisor at the Brooklyn Public Library, she works to bring a sense of community ownership and interaction to the library. She is creative, passionate about connecting library patrons to the services they really need, and a true believer in the ability of the library to change people's lives and communities for the better.

4.6.1 Takeaways

- If the event that you want to attend does not currently exist, why not create it yourself or with like-minded colleagues?
- Bigger does not mean better. It usually means more expensive, and it sometimes means alienating.
- A lot can be done with a DIY approach, volunteers, and sponsorships. Be prepared to work hard but never be afraid to ask for help.

References

Allied Media Projects. (n.d.-a). 200th[th] Annual Allied Media Conference (2018). Retrieved from https://www.alliedmedia.org/amc/2018.

Allied Media Projects. (n.d.-b). *How we organize the Allied Media Conference zine, Vol. 1*. Retrieved from https://www.alliedmedia.org/sites/default/files/how_we_organize_the_amc_zine_vol_1.pdf.

Allied Media Projects. (n.d.-c). Media-based organizing. Retrieved from https://www.alliedmedia.org/media-based-organizing.

Allied Media Projects. (n.d.-d). Radical Libraries, Archives, and Museums Track. Retrieved from https://www.alliedmedia.org/amc2018/rad-libraries-archives-museums-track.

Amelia Bloomer Project. (n.d.). Amelia bloomer project: Recommended feminist literature from birth to 18. Retrieved from https://ameliabloomer.wordpress.com/about/amelia-bloomer-project-book-criteria/.

Bell, G. S. (2006). Gathering at the waters: Embracing our spirits, telling our stories. In *Proceedings of the 1st National Joint Conference of Librarians of Color*, Dallas, Texas.

Cassell, K. (Ed.) (1980, September). Women in libraries. *Newsletter of the ALA/SRRT — Feminist Task Force* (Vol. 10, No. 1, pp. 1−8).

Comito, L. (2019). *Tech for all: Moving beyond the digital divide*. Lanham, MD: Rowman and Littlefield.

Comito, L., Geraci, A., & Zabriskie, C. (2012). *Grassroots library advocacy*. Chicago: American Library Association.

Corey, S. (2000). *You forgot your skirt, Amelia Bloomer: A very improper story*. New York: Scholastic Press, on June.

Eberhart, G. M. (2017, January 21). Librarians on the march. *American Libraries*. Retrieved from https://americanlibrariesmagazine.org/blogs/the-scoop/librarians-on-the-march/.

Feminist Task Force. (2005). Historical notes. Retrieved from http://www.libr.org/ftf/history.html.

Figueroa, M. (2012). Flake, Myracle, Otsuka join Joint Conference of Librarians of Color. *ALA News*. Retrieved from http://www.ala.org/news/press-releases/2012/02/flake-myracle-otsuka-join-joint-conference-librarians-color.

Fleming, R., & McBride, K. (2017). How we speak, how we think, what we do: Leading intersectional feminist conversations in libraries. In S. Lew, & B. Yousef (Eds.), *Feminists among us: Resistance and advocacy in library leadership* (p. 119). Sacramento, CA: Library Juice Press.

Gay, Lesbian, Bisexual, and Transgender Round Table. (2019a). GLBTRT award for political activism. Retrieved from http://www.ala.org/rt/glbtrt/awards/political-activism.

Gay, Lesbian, Bisexual, and Transgender Round Table. (2019b). Larry Romans Mentorship Award. Retrieved from http://www.ala.org/rt/glbtrt/awards/larry-romans.

Gay, Lesbian, Bisexual, and Transgender Round Table. (2019c). The Newlen-Symons Award for Excellence in Serving the GLBT Community. Retrieved from http://www.ala.org/rt/glbtrt/awards/newlen-symons-award-excellence-serving-glbt-community.

Gay, Lesbian, Bisexual, and Transgender Round Table Newsletter. (2011). GLBTRT updates name-changes -- "transgendered" to -- "transgender". *GLBTRT Newsletter: Gay, Lesbian, Bisexual, & Transgendered Round Table, 23*(1), 1.

Harrington, S. (2017). Feminist Task Force news. *SRRT Newsletter Social Responsibilities Round Table, 200*, 5.

Harrington, S. (2018). Feminist Task Force news. *SRRT Newsletter Social Responsibilities Round Table, 203*, 4.

Hildenbrand, S. (2000). Library feminism and library women's history: Activism and scholarship, equity and culture. *Libraries & Culture, 35*(1), 51−65.

Jenson, K. (Ed.), (2017). *Here we are: Feminism for the real world*. Algonquin: Chapel Hill, NC.

Joint Council of Librarians of Color. (2019). About. Retrieved from https://www.jclcinc. org/about/.

Kagan, A. (2015). *Progressive library organizations: A worldwide history*. Jefferson, NC: McFarland.

Klinenberg, E. (2018). *Palaces for the people: How social infrastructure can help Fight inequality, polarization, and the decline of civic life*. New York, NY: Crown.

Kostelecky, S. (2018). Joint conference of librarians of color meeting − gathering all peoples: Embracing culture & community. *Against the Grain, 30*(6), 57.

McElroy, K. (2017). A woman's work is never done: Reference outside the library. In M. T. Accardi (Ed.), *The feminist reference desk: Concepts, critiques, and conversations* (pp. 85−100). Sacramento, CA: Library Juice Press.

Miller, R., & Bardales, A. (2006). Better together: The joint conference. *Library Journal, 131*(19), 34−35.

Morales, M. (2012). Joint conference of librarians of color (JCLC). *Progressive Librarian, 91*−94.

Morales, M. (2018). Joint conference of librarians of color 2018. Retrieved from http://www.jclcinc.org/conference/2018/wp-content/uploads/2018/09/JCLC-Fact-Sheet-2018.09.04-LPL-Edits.pdf.

Morales, M. (2019). Awards and scholarships press release. Retrieved from http://www.jclcinc.org/conference/2018/awards-and-scholarships-press-release/.

PAG. (2006). First joint conference of librarians of color: Historic gathering draws hundreds to Dallas. *American Libraries*, 20−21.

SinhaRoy, S. (2012). Librarians of color meet in Kansas. *American Libraries, 43*(11/12), 17.

Socha, K. (2019). Under consideration for March 2019. Over the Rainbow Books. Retrieved from https://www.glbtrt.ala.org/overtherainbow/.

Urban Librarians Unite. (n.d.-a). Libraries serve refugees: Resources by librarians—For everyone. Retrieved from https://refugeelibraries.org/.

Urban Librarians Unite. (n.d-b). NYC elected officials. Retrieved from https://urban librariansunite.org/nyc-elected-officials/.

Urban Librarians Unite. (n.d-c). Social events. Retrieved from https://urbanlibrariansunite.org/our-work/social-events/.

Urban Libraries Conference. (n.d.). Home. Retrieved from https://www.urbanlibrarians conference.org/.

Women's March (2019). About us: Mission and principles. Retrieved from https://womensmarch.com/mission-and-principles.

CHAPTER FIVE

CODA

The existence of progressive and radical library and information projects is certainly nothing new or even recent. Kagan (2015) has written extensively about them in his *Progressive Library Groups: A Worldwide History*, as well as his annual updates to that book. Furthermore, the library and information professions have long produced many influential individuals considered progressive or radical. For example, Eric Moon, librarian and founder of Scarecrow Press was, according to Kister (2002), "instrumental in exposing and eliminating institutional racism in American librarianship, and in democratizing the ALA, hitherto the preserve of a narrow, conservative elite" (p. 405). Public librarian Ruth Brown's advocacy of African Americans likely led to her being labeled a communist and fired from her job in 1950 (Robbins, 2000). British-Kenyan librarian Shiraz Durrani has struggled against Western imperialism since the 1970s, and his writings have done much to situate our understanding of the role of libraries in the context of post-colonialism. Audre Lorde and Lao-Tzu were both library workers at one time, suggesting that libraries attract radical change agents across cultures and across time.

It was our great privilege and delight, therefore, to not only discover 30 transformative information organizations, initiatives, and programs, but also to encounter the individual change agents associated with those projects. The profiles in this book are the result of a two-year process that included many long form interviews, research, and much writing. This was an oftentimes-grueling process requiring careful attention to planning and logistics. It was, however, an immensely rewarding endeavor, providing the authors with the opportunity to learn about a wide-range of inspiring projects, hearing first hand from those directly involved. Everyone that we spoke with was deeply invested in what they were doing and passionate about the capacity for people to change society with information, and hence the necessity to safeguard and promote people's access to information, as well as their ability to create and use it freely. The book writing process allowed its authors to understand that, while the projects considered may appear to be greatly different from each other in terms of specific missions, activities, and scale, they share

Transformative Library and Information Work.
DOI: https://doi.org/10.1016/B978-0-08-103011-0.00009-5
© 2020 Elsevier Ltd.
All rights reserved.

commonalities. Funding, or the lack thereof, reared its head repeatedly over the course of the interviews. The most frequent concept to assert itself over the course of our research, however, was that of *community*. The word "community," in fact, appears in this book almost 300 times, that is nearly twice per page.

All information projects, regardless of whether or not they are progressive or conservative, radical or stolidly neoliberal, see that community is the backbone of their work. Without community, there is no point. We discovered that what sets the projects profiled here apart from the hegemonic/dominant information institutions—e.g., the majority of the academic libraries and government-funded public libraries—is that the counter-hegemonic projects recognize that the modern information institution hinges on relationships, that the modern information project is, in fact, intricately *composed of relationships*. These projects explicitly recognized that the library (or the archive, or the museum. . .) is much more than just edifice; it is a web of things and ideas extending far beyond physical walls. The information project, at least the successful information project, is the one that has become essentially synonymous with community, or at the very least, an organic appendage to community. It serves as a focal point, provides cohesion, and creates a sense of belonging. Just as communities evolve, successful information projects must evolve with them, supporting the evolving needs of community, fighting for access, navigating controversy, and yes, perennially hunting down sources of funding. We found during the course of our investigation that every one of the transformative projects in this book share the fact that its team members are *profoundly conscious* of these axioms: information projects are relationships; relationships always change, and, to be successful, progressive and radical information work must be open to change and eager to effect it. Repeatedly we encountered a sense of purpose that was palpable, inspiring, and infectious.

References

Kagan, A. (2015). *Progressive library organizations: A worldwide history*. Jefferson, NC: McFarland.

Kister, K. F. (2002). *Eric Moon: The life and library times*. Jefferson, NC: McFarland & Company.

Robbins, L. S. (2000). *The dismissal of Miss Ruth Brown: Civil rights, censorship, and the American library*. Norman, OK: University of Oklahoma Press.

Index

Made in United States
North Haven, CT
29 August 2022

23410367R00089